D1063170

LEAVING TRAILS OF LIGHT
AND TOILET PAPER

REFLECTIONS OF A DEPRESSED OPTIMIST ON FAMILY, LOVE, AND LIGHT

MARY LILLEY-THOMPSON

Printed in the United States of America

Published in Hellertown, PA

Cover design by Kristen Williams

Library of Congress Control Number 2022903797

ISBN 978-1-952481-88-8

2 4 6 8 10 9 7 5 3 1

For more information or to place bulk orders, contact the publisher at Jennifer@BrightCommunications.net.

This book is dedicated to my family,
especially my husband, Bill,
and daughter, Jessica

CONTENTS

INTRODUCTION

"If there is light in the soul, there will be beauty in the person. If there is beauty in the person, there will be harmony in the house. If there is harmony in the house, there will be order in the nation. If there is order in the nation, there will be peace in the world."
—Chinese proverb

I believe that laughter, humor, leaving trails of Light, radiating Light from within, having a great therapist and being on the right medications can get us through the rough waters of life. In this book, I've shared some rough waters of my life. You might have moments when you say to yourself, "OMG, that's me!" Or, "That sounds like my mother!" Or, "I've been divorced, too." In many ways, we may be very much alike. I've discovered time and again that these aspects of beliefs were critical to my survival, and more importantly, my thriving.

If you are stuck in survival mode and you want to thrive, this book is for you. If you are thriving, this book will underscore how you came to thrive, even though our journeys may be slightly different. You will rejoice in yourself! While reading this book, I hope that you'll have some laughs, and you'll shed some tears. It's good if you do both. My life has been made up of many tears and bouts of laughter.

Without knowing sorrow, there is no joy. My hope is that you will come away from reading this book believing that there are Lights at the end of your tunnels, that you shine Light from within, that you'll find a great therapist and medications, if needed, and that you will know how to leave trails of Light for others.

You might be wondering why I capitalize the word "Light." Some folks like to think of God as Light. Light is part of my being. It's the Light within that is my very best self. As you read this book, you will come to realize the importance of Light. May the Light that you find in this book be a beacon for you.

PART I

DYNAMIC DYSFUNCTION

"People talk about dysfunctional families. I've never seen any other kind."
—Sue Grafton

1

THE MATRIARCH

/ˈmātrēˌärk/
noun
a woman who is the head of a family or tribe.
"in some cultures the mother proceeds to the status of a
matriarch"
an older woman who is powerful within a family or
organization.
"a domineering matriarch"

My mother was the domineering matriarch of our family. She loved to be in control of herself, others, and every situation. She was detail oriented when it came to planning an agenda for a meeting for an organization of which she was president, a list for a dinner party, packing a picnic lunch, and writing a family to-do list. She was organized with her house, her pantry, her clothing, her shoes, her drawers, her junk drawer, and when she would have sex–every Saturday night. God forbid, if Mother couldn't control everything.

In the early fall of 1943, she auditioned for the Metropolitan Opera chorus, and she was accepted–until they found out she was pregnant. So she lost control of that. And I took too long to be born. She lost control of that, too. She never let me forget it!

When any of us children would be sick, Mother had a rule that we had to be well in three days. After that, Mother would make us go back to school, and she would stop being a nursemaid to us–no more alcohol back rubs or meals in bed. When we were actually sick for more than three days with measles or chickenpox, she resented it. And when my brother Billy contracted polio, she really lost control. But she did allow him to be sick for six days.

Growing up, I enjoyed adventures. I'd be wont to wander off without saying anything to anyone. When I was five years old, while living in Youngstown, Ohio, my mommy decided I needed a note on me before I went out to play. The note said, "Send Mary back home by 5:30 pm," with our phone number to call in case of emergencies.

Back then, I was a little chunky and always hungry it seemed. I still am. Chunky and hungry.

One afternoon, I decided to go searching for food at my friends' homes. I told Mommy I was going out to play, so she pinned the note on me. Off I went. I started at the Kleckner's house. I played with Janet for a while and asked if we could have a snack. Her mom made Kool-Aid for us and gave us some peanut butter on slices of soft, white bread. We folded them over and gobbled them up.

"Please," I asked for another.

"You don't really need another, Mary. You're a little chubby already," Janet's mom said.

That really stung. I left quickly after that. I didn't want Janet or her mom to see me cry.

I headed to the neighborhood grocery store. The people who owned it were Greek and lived upstairs. I always smelled food wafting down the stairway from their apartment. I'd never been there, but I knew the people, so I thought they might have some food. I went up the stairs and knocked on their door. The owner's wife, Mrs. Koutonous, answered the door wearing a house dress and apron. That was a good sign.

"Do you happen to have any food for a little girl like me?" I asked, in my most pathetic sounding voice.

"Sure! Come on in!" Mrs. Koutonous said.

She fed me Greek meatballs that were so yummy I still salivate when I think of them. She called my mother and told her the story of my visit. Mommy walked to the store to get me. She was really apologetic to Mrs. Koutonous, and then she took my hand, which she held extremely tightly until it hurt, and we left. Mommy walked very fast, and I could hardly keep up with her. When she was angry, she moved fast and heavy-footed. Always did.

"I can't believe you did that. What's she going to think?" my mother kept saying. She'd lost control of me, and she was embarrassed and mad. When we got home, she got the hairbrush and spanked me. "Don't you EVER do anything like that again! Begging for food! Promise me! How dare you! You're just a pig!" she said.

I promised her, through tears. That was the beginning of my hating myself and my body. I had hit one of my first patches of rough water.

I went to my room where my sister, Marcia, was reading, threw myself on my bed, and sobbed. In between sobs I said, "I hate her. I'm going to run away from home some day."

"You really don't mean that. You'll feel better soon," Marcia said. She went back to reading.

But I didn't feel better for many, many years.

One day, my friends and I were playing with some kids, and someone called me "fatty." I ran inside the house crying to Mommy, blubbering out what had happened. She gave me the lesson about sticks and stones, but it didn't comfort me. Mommy gave me a snack of cookies and milk and told me I'd feel better.

I took that literally. It translated into the beginning of my obsession with food. I felt I'd never get enough to feel better.

My mommy had an elegant side. Her makeup was perfectly applied, and her accessories all matched. When we attended church, all of us girls wore white gloves and hats. Marcia and I loved dressing up, and Mommy was an excited participant in that process. She shared her entire wardrobe with us, even her cocktail dresses and high-heeled shoes. She applied our makeup and taught us how to put lipstick on without a mirror. I loved this side of my mother—when she was having fun with us!

When it was bedtime, and we didn't want to go to bed, she would pretend that we were strippers and sing that stripping song. That's how she tricked us into getting undressed and putting our nighties on!

Back in the late forties, Mommy was involved with the Youngstown Playhouse as both an actress and the costume mistress. To access the costumes, we had to climb an eight-foot ladder up to a two-foot-wide platform. It was scary, because once we were on the platform, it would be easy to fall off. For Halloween each year, Marcia and I were able to pick our costumes from the collection.

One year, Mommy insisted that we climb the ladder to retrieve our costumes. She had pulled the Minnie Mouse costume for me. It was my favorite. It had a papier-mâché head! I was scared to death to climb the ladder, but Mommy insisted again. She was balanced on the ledge, and she said that she didn't want to climb up and down that ladder any more than she had to. I mustered the courage, climbed up, and grabbed the costume. Climbing backward down the ladder was tricky, but I made it back down. It was all worth it because I won the first prize for the best costume in the town's Halloween parade! Mom felt proud and in control!

My parents entertained a lot. Those were the days of cocktail, dinner, and bridge parties. According to all their friends, my parents were fabulous hosts.

When I was seven years old, I loved helping Mommy get ready for her guests, especially in the kitchen where I could sample the food. She was famous for her lobster dip. My favorite party foods were that dip and Bologna Stack-Ups, both of which I was allowed to make.

My mom would put all the ingredients for the lobster dip out on the counter. My job was to mix them all together. Some of the ingredients I remember included: cream cheese, sour cream, chopped scallions, lemon juice, and lobster meat. Of course, I had to sample it.

To make Bologna Stack-ups, I spread softened cream cheese in between 10 slices of bologna until the stack was complete—with no cream cheese on the top layer. I would put the stacks in the fridge to chill overnight, then cut each stack like a pie into 16 slices. Recently, I saw this on Facebook as one of those horrible 1950s recipes. I loved it because I loved both bologna, which we called baloney, and cream cheese!

And then there was the dip jar. When Mommy served crudites for appetizers, she always served it with her special dip. It slightly varied from one time to the next because the ingredients would change slightly each time. The dip began when a jar of mayonnaise was three-quarters empty. She would add stuff to that, which included, but was not limited to, sour cream, more mayo, always sweet relish, maybe a little ketchup, chopped onion, and miscellaneous seasonings. This was served in a small dish at the center of the crudite arrangement. I don't recall that we had the "do not double dip" rule in our household.

When the party was over, Mom put the leftover dip back into the dip jar for the next time when all of this would be repeated. Years later, my sister-in-law Nancy called our attention to the dip jar and its partially used contents! From then on, we made jokes about the dip jar, and I'm not sure that I ever ate any again!

One evening in July, while getting ready for a cocktail party, Mommy got impatient with Marcia and me because we couldn't see what had to be done, which infuriated her. She started stomping around. It was just about time for the guests to come, and she started barking orders at us.

"Mary, put these napkins on the table! You should be able to see what needs to be done!" she yelled at me.

"Marcia, the plates! Put those plates on the table. Can't you two hurry up?" Mom scolded my sister.

Then the doorbell rang. My mom went to the door, and we could hear her sweet voice welcoming her guests in. She sounded so nice. She came back to the kitchen to tell us to go to bed.

"Can't we stay up and see everyone?" I asked.

"Absolutely not!" Mom whisper-screamed.

"Just for a little bit?" we whined.

"Get to your room right now!" Mom yelled.

Obviously, this was no time for the stripping game! The doorbell rang again.

Marcia and I trudged off to the bedroom and put on our nighties. We did our bathroom routine of brushing teeth and crawled in our beds, still pouting a bit.

As Mommy and Daddy did every night, they came to the bedroom door to sing to us and ask, "What was the nicest thing that happened to you today," all just loud enough for the guests to hear. When it was my turn to tell the nicest thing that happened today, I said, with tears welling up, "You talk so mean to us and so nice to your friends. We're your children, and you didn't even borned them."

"Oh, don't be so silly! Go to sleep now. Goodnight," Mommy said, turned off the light, and closed the door.

Marcia and I stayed awake a while. She read under the covers with a flashlight, and I cried some more and played with my dolls in the dark. We then got up, quietly sneaked to the door, and opened it a couple of inches so we could hear what was going on.

Everyone was laughing and having a good time. We heard the clinking of glasses and someone was making a toast to Ruth and Bill, our parents. We assumed they were toasting them as great hosts. We listened for another few minutes, then got bored and went to bed.

The next day, Mommy and Daddy told Marcia and me that we were going to have a new addition to the family—a new baby brother or sister. I was beside myself, so excited with this news! We were going to have to wait until September for the event to happen. I could hardly wait!

When I was 11 years old, I got the sex speech from my mom. It went something like this: "The man fertilizes the woman's egg just like we fertilize the garden. The egg grows like a flower does and becomes a baby inside the woman's body." Then Mom stopped and waited for me to respond.

"How does the fertilizer get into the woman's body?" I asked.

"When two people love each other, they make love, and it happens then," Mom answered.

"What happens?" I asked.

My mom immediately got angry and said, "It's not any of your business!"

I felt I'd been slapped. I was dumbfounded. At that moment, I realized that something had happened between my parents in order for Mom to get pregnant with Billy.

"Oh. Okay," I said.

I decided to ask Marcia what that was all about. Marcia read and was smart about everything, and I knew she'd tell me. Well, she did, and I didn't believe her because I couldn't figure out how it all worked together.

It must have worked for Mom and Dad again, because my brother Steve was born when I was 11. I'd received enough information from Marcia, books, and my friend Gerry, who knew everything about sex. I was embarrassed to think that everyone knew that my parents had had sex four times in their marriage. I knew they hadn't done THAT just for the pleasure of it–until several years later when Marcia explained that people did it just for fun!

When I was 12, I discovered my body in the studio in the basement in our house on the Sharon-Mercer Road in Charleston, Pennsylvania. What I didn't know would happen, because Marcia didn't mention it, was that I would climax. I was shocked. It was glorious. It repeated itself three or four times. I guess I was pretty horny. I also was ashamed and horrified because I believed that no one else in the world had ever done what I did. I believed that I would need to keep this my secret until I went to my grave. I think I was horny for the next 55 years. Luckily, I learned to accept that fact, and it was okay.

As I entered my teen years, I found it easier to confide in Mother. I wanted to please her, but I often found myself having strong opinions of things that would set her off. This included not wanting to do my chores in the morning before I could do anything fun with friends. I wondered, why couldn't I just do the chores on that day at any time? Also, I wouldn't see things that had to be done, like setting the table for dinner, sweeping the kitchen floor after supper, emptying waste baskets when they were full, and the list went on. However, I always did what she asked.

One time, I told her that I felt like Cinderella and that the only reason she wanted children was to do her chores! She didn't like that and slapped me across the face. I also got slapped for rolling my eyes or deeply sighing when assigned a chore. That was our generation's equivalent of saying "whatever."

Early on, I learned not to show my negative emotions or express opinions. If my siblings and I were upset or angry, we were sent to our rooms and told to stay there until we could come out with smiles on our faces. My mother was desperate to be in control of me during my teen years. She had a big job. I found lots of ways to rebel.

In my teen years, I thought Mom was a phony. When she wanted to impress someone, she softened her Rs like actors in 1930s movies–a quasi British accent, but not that affected.

My mother was a born leader, organizer, committee woman, and director–roles in which she could be in control. Mother planned all her meals a week in advance and had dinner on the table every night. During dinner, she wanted to control what and how much we ate and the subjects of conversation.We were rewarded for cleaning our plates and punished when we didn't want to try the three required bites.

Poor Marcia. She was a lot pickier than I was, and many nights she sat at the table until bedtime because she wouldn't bend. I admired her for that. As I think about it now, I realize it was her way of taking control even if she went to bed hungry. I would never go to bed hungry.

It took me many years of therapy to get over my mother's control over me. Thanks to my first counselor, Mildred Shagam, I learned I had a lot to work on. Someone who knew my mother's true nature once said, "Your mother is the kind of person who could stab you in the back with a feather and watch you bleed to death."

The first time I stood up against my Mother was when I was in my 30s and left my family and moved to Allentown with a promotion and job transfer. It was my way of running away from home like I promised Marcia all those years earlier! It wasn't until I was in my 50s that I was able to completely separate myself from her control. My weight became an issue of struggle for control, and every time my husband, Bill, and I visited my parents, my mother mentioned my weight or what and how much I was eating.

At the time, I weighed almost 300 pounds. I was in business for myself, doing corporate presentations on professional image and nonverbal communication. I felt quite self-assured and confident about who I was—in spite of my weight. I was a nationally known keynote speaker, yet my father told me, "I don't understand how you have any credibility being as fat as you are."

I was so angry with my parents that before we made our next trip to Pittsburgh, where they lived, I called them.

"We're so anxious to see you," Mother said.

"I'm anxious to see you, too, but I need to tell you something first," I replied. "When we're out there, I do not want you or Dad to mention my weight or what or how much I'm eating at all. If you do, Bill and I will no longer stay with you when we visit. Do you understand?"

The hives had come back around my neck while I said this. Rough water. That was the most assertive I'd ever been with my mother. She gasped dramatically.

"You have no idea how much you've hurt me by saying that!" she said, with a tear in her voice. You see, it was all about her.

"It's too bad that you choose to feel that way," I said. "Do I have your promise?"

"I suppose, if you feel that strongly about it, we won't say anything," my mother said. "Mary, just remember, you have such a pretty face."

I was nonplussed. I said, "See you soon," and hung up.

I was so mad! I was a mess.

I updated Bill, and he hugged me and told me he was really proud that I'd been able to talk with her the way I did. I was proud of myself, too. My parents never mentioned my weight or my eating patterns again.

My mother's control over me ended because I had grown and stopped letting her push my buttons. She had also grown, and a wonderful thing happened. From the time I was in my mid 50s, our relationship became one of a loving mother and daughter who had also become friends. We enjoyed spending time with each other. When she died, we were at peace with each other. Two years before she died, in May 2000, I wrote this prose.

Lessons from Mom's Purse

I loved Mom's purse. It was the essence of her. By the time I was five years old, she trusted me to occasionally go into that magic place to get 50 cents to buy milk and bread at the store around the corner. Tokens of my mother's elegance and style were in her purse.

Perfume: She always carried a handkerchief that smelled of the perfume she wore. I think it was Chanel No. 5 or WindSong. The hankies were hand embroidered or crocheted lovelies, which had been given to her by friends over the years. They were used only once, then washed and always ironed.

Peppermint: It was, and still is, the only flavor of gum and mints that Mother really likes. She ALWAYS had gum or peppermints. You chewed gum to make your breath fresh while you were on your way to a PTA meeting, tea, concert, choir practice, or bridge game. You never chewed with your mouth open, and you spit the gum out in the original gum wrapper just before you arrived at the event.

Cigarettes: In the 30s, 40s and 50s, when it was the most sophisticated thing to do, Mom smoked unfiltered Chesterfields. She wore red nail polish and often would have to carefully pick a tiny piece of tobacco from the tip of her tongue. Unlike Dad, Mother never spit.

Red lipstick: Always red. It had the scent of wax and cherries–or at least I thought it did. Mother would encourage my sister and me to play dress up and wear her lipstick, which I'd learned to keep inside the lines.

Mom is now legally blind. One day while I was helping her at the Social Security office, she handed me her purse to find her card. I opened it up, and all these childhood memories washed over me with the same two scents: peppermint and old perfume—except now the mints are sugar free and the perfume scent is Chantilly.

I look at Mother, and I am flooded with emotions. I learned so much from her purse.

She encouraged **creativity** by showing me how to "pretend" with lipstick.

She taught me **compassion** by wiping my tears with those delicate handkerchiefs.

Cleanliness was taught when she would spit on her handkerchief and rub dirt off of my face.

I learned certain **social graces:** Chew gum for fresh breath and don't spit in public.

I was abruptly brought back to reality when my mom said, "While you're looking for the card, would you please get me a peppermint?"

I gave her a mint and a hug and said, "Thanks for all the lessons you taught me, Mom!"

She smiled and said, "I'm not sure where that came from, but you're welcome."

A postscript: I read this story to Mother on Mother's Day the year before she passed away. She was horrified when she heard the cigarettes entry!

"I never smoked!" she said.

Then she realized that she'd been in total denial about ever smoking. Mom never dwelled on the negative. She'd smoked for more than 30 years and finally quit when she was in her 50s.

"I was so ashamed that I'd smoked—such a filthy habit and what an awful example for you kids," she moaned.

When I told her that I was going to publish this on my website, she was mortified. I told her I'd write this postscript to announce her shame. She said that would be good.

2

THE PATRIARCH

/ˈpātrēˌärk/

noun

1.the male head of a family or tribe.

I t was Father's Day 2000 when I wrote the following essay, Brewsky and Grass, as a gift to my dad. Unfortunately, because of his dementia, for the most part, I feared he might not understand everything I was reading to him, which saddened me. That was until I finished it, and he looked at me and said, "Miss Mary." That may have been the only thing he heard or understood, but it was enough for me.

I wept.

It's written in the present tense so that you can get a feel for my voice at different ages.

Brewsky and Grass

August 1948—the Ellenwood Avenue House, Youngstown, Pennsylvania

I can hear Daddy cutting the grass out back. He's using a push mower. It's very hot. The back screen door slams shut. (Mommy doesn't like that.)

"Time for a beer," my Dad says. He goes to the fridge and takes out a brown bottle. He sighs as he sits down at the kitchen table and pries off the bottle cap. Some of the white frothy stuff comes out of the top. He slurps it just in time.

"Now that sure tastes great, Miss Mary."

I'm four years old. Daddy smells like freshly cut green grass. He winks at me.

"May I please have a sip?" I ask.

"Sure can," my dad said.

The beer tastes fizzy and silly and yucky all at the same time. I am happy that Daddy shared it with me. I love being with my daddy. I really love it when he calls me "Miss Mary."

July, 1955–the Sharon-Mercer Road house, Mercer, Pennsylvania

It's 95 degrees outside.

"Please take this beer out to your dad," my mom says, as she pries open a beer bottle. "I'm sure he'll appreciate the break."

I run outside with the bottle and shout to Daddy, but he's mowing way out by the road and can't hear me. Our front yard is an acre.

I hop on my three-speed bike with the hand brakes and

ride down the driveway, holding on to the sweating bottle with my left hand and waving to get Daddy's attention with my right. My front wheel catches a piece of slag. My front tire slides to the right, and I fly off my bike, still holding the bottle in my left hand.

Daddy sees this and runs to me to be sure that I'm okay. The bottle is frothing, and he grabs it to catch the cold foam just in time. My knee is skinned, and I hold back the tears to be brave. I feel proud that I lost only a couple of ounces of beer.

My dad winks at me and asks if I want a sip. I wipe the gravel off the lip of the bottle and sip. It tastes cold, wet, and yucky. My dad wipes my knee off with his old sweaty towel. Then he kisses my knee and says it will be fine. He downs the beer and thanks me as he hands me the empty bottle.

He pulls the mower's rope starter and swears when he can't get the mower going.

"Dagnamit!" he shouts after the third try.

On the fourth pull, the mower starts and my dad winks at me again. I take the empty bottle back to the house in the basket on my bike. I work up real tears for Mom. I think she'll put iodine on my knee. But she will blow on it.

This summer, I'm 11-1/2 years old. It's the best summer ever. I spend my time practicing cartwheels, playing jacks, twirling a baton, playing with my little brothers, Billy and four-month-old Steve, building a hide-away with my best friend, Terry, and riding my bike. I'm the only person I know who has a three-speed bike with hand brakes. My daddy taught me how to ride a bike and how to swim and dive. I feel free when I'm in the water and on my bike. My daddy gives me wings. The world is mine.

June 1961–the East Market Street house, Mercer, Pennsylvania

On Saturday morning, my dad is once again cutting the grass in the backyard. We're both hot and a little cranky.

"I think it's time for a break and a beer," my dad says.

"I think it's time that I take the car to the swimming pool," I reply. He chuckles and says, "Well, Miss Mary, you'll have to ride your bike because I need to go do some work at the office."

We walk inside where my mom is making an arrangement of cut flowers from her garden. Dad grabs a brewsky from the fridge and asks what's for supper later on.

"You're doing hamburgers on the grill!" my mom says.

"My favorite, especially with cheddar cheese!" my dad replies.

I grab a glass of freshly brewed iced tea and guzzle it down. I still had to choose another chore from the Saturday family to-do list, and I choose to mow the front yard, which is under shade trees.

"Thanks, Miss Mary! Now I don't have to do it," my dad says and winks.

I'm 17 years old. I just graduated from high school with high honors and the graduate drama and music awards. I'm on top of the world!

I hop on my old three-speed bike and head to the pool where a bunch of my friends will be hanging out. I know I will have limited time with them before I'm off to State College, Pennsylvania, to spend the summer with my wonderful sister, Marcia, and her husband, Dick. I'm going to become an aunt for the first time ever, and I am thrilled about it. Then, in late August, I'm heading by train to Lincoln,

Nebraska, to the University of Nebraska. I'm seeing my life as an adventure!

May 2000–Presbyterian Senior Care, Woodside Place, Oakmont, Pennsylvania

It's an unusually warm day for May. Dad sits in his wheelchair and looks out the window of his room in the Alzheimer's/Dementia Unit. He's watching a guy on a riding mower cut the grass at the fourth tee of the Oakmont Country Club. He looks up at me.

"You know…," he starts to say, then stops.

He forgets. He looks back outside and smiles.

"How about you and I go for a ride in the green car?" I ask.

He brightens and says, "That'd be great."

"How about we go get a cheeseburger and fries?" I ask.

"And a brewsky, too!" he says and winks at me.

This is more than Dad has said in weeks. I learn from the nurse that you can buy beer on draft to go. Kewl. We head over Coxcomb Hill and past townhouse developments, a fancy-dancy retirement community, and the Allegheny River. Dad reads most of the signs along the way aloud.

"Wow, that's the river," he says.

We pull up to the beer-and-burger joint. As I watch a guy pour ice cold draft beer into a squatty quart-sized plastic jug and seal it, I wonder just how we're going to handle this in the car–driving with an opened alcohol container in a moving vehicle being illegal and all.

I carry the jug to the car. As I get in, I hold it up to Dad and say, "Brewsky!"

He laughs and makes a yuck face. I think he thought it was urine. It actually does look like urine. Anyway, I rummage through my backseat and find a huge, 32-ounce plastic cup. I pour some of the beer from the jug into the cup perfectly so nothing spills and the head isn't too thick. I hand Dad the cup, and he looks at me as if I'm crazy.

"Drink up," I say.

I'm still wondering how we're going to drive off with this opened jug of beer in the car. My dad takes the cup and takes a sip. Hmmmmmmmmm, good, is the expression on his face. He raises his eyebrows and smacks his lips. Our burgers and fries are delivered to the car. I decide to bite the bullet and start the car. I put the cap on the jug and sit it, still containing quite a bit of beer, under my left leg and hope it doesn't roll around too much. Dad smiles and keeps sipping.

It's hot, so I tell my dad that we're going to find a cool spot where we can eat our lunch. I'm not sure where that will be, but I know I'll find something. We drive by a condo development with a lovely tree-lined entrance. I turn in.

"Where are we going?" Dad asks.

"I'm not sure, but it's okay," I reply.

My Dad keeps sipping–and smiling.

I wind around the development and find a parking place shaded by a lovely maple tree and lilac bush. I pull into the spot.

"Whose tree …" my dad asks. He forgets to finish his question, but I know what he's asking.

"I don't know who lives here, but they sure have a pretty tree, and this is where we're going to eat lunch," I say.

I turn off the engine, leaving the ignition on so that we

can listen to Poulenc's "Sonata for Clarinet and Piano." Dad devours his cheeseburger and sips some more brewsky.

He looks at me and asks, "Do you …," as he holds the cup over to me.

"No thanks, Dad, that's your brewsky. Besides, I don't even like beer. The last beer I had was the sip you gave me when I skinned my knee at the Sharon-Mercer Road house," I say.

My dad has no idea what I am talking about, and he just nods his head with a half smile. I pour him some more beer after he finishes his burger. It is good to see him eat. He is six feet tall and weighs only 149 pounds.

So, here we are: illegally parked (probably), illegally driving with an open container of brewsky (definitely), listening to Poulenc and a distant lawn mower (surely). I can smell the lilacs, and I think of my daughter, Jessica. And there's Dad, just smiling. It was a perfect moment in time.

On the drive back to Woodside, we stop at my daughter's house so that my dad can see his great granddaughter, Kate. I bring her out to the car and hand her to Dad. There they are–Great GrandPop and Kate. He is smiling, and Kate is smiling back.

"She's a fine baby," he says.

And, of course, I'm crying.

Once we arrive back at Woodside, I try to help Dad transfer from the green car to his wheelchair, but he's so looped that I can't stand him up. It takes a nurse's aid helping me to get him out of the car. My dad is still smiling, but now he's looking rather sleepy. I'm sure he'll sleep well. I kiss him goodbye, and he looks at me with an expression that tells me he is wondering, "I know I know you, but I'm not sure why you're here."

"I love you," I say.

"Thanks, Miss Mary," he replies. Then he winks.

I love being with my dad. I love his essence. He taught me how to be silly and how to play. He gave me my wings, and now he's the wind beneath them. I love you, Dad. Happy Father's Day.

I had a very complex relationship with my dad from my teen years until I was in my 30s. When Jessica was a preteen, we had almost no relationship at all, but that's a story for a little later. That said, my early years were idyllic, and his senior years were beyond precious. He loved me unconditionally at those times.

My dad worked hard and played hard. He adored my mother, Ruth Johnson Hammond. His license plate said RJH-1. They were playful with each other. I often saw him pat her on the butt. They hugged and kissed in front of us kids.

When I was quite little, I would sometimes want to be a part of that love, so I would wriggle myself in between them when they were smooching. They would make room for me, and I would say the word "loooove." In my early years, I felt unconditional love from them. They would say I lit up a room when I entered, and they called me Mary Sunshine. Life was good.

When I was very young, Daddy was always up for a new adventure! He took me tobogganing once at the Tam O'Shanter golf course in Sharon, Pennsylvania. They had a perfect hill for sledding and tobogganing. I must have been eight or nine years old, and this was a new experience for us. He wanted me to feel safe and at the same time enjoy the adventure of it.

"You sit here–in the front. It's the most exciting place to sit!" he said.

I had some trepidation about that, considering I had a bad sledding accident when I was four years old. We'd gone sledding, and Dad decided I could handle going down the hill by myself. He gave me a push off, but he hadn't told me how to steer. I crashed into a concrete bridge, hitting my left eyebrow area. An ER visit and stitches ensued. I still have the scar. But I was lucky.

Back to the toboggan. My dad reassured me by squeezing in behind me and holding on to the ropes to steer. His knees hugged me in place, and I felt safe. Six more people climbed into the toboggan, and we were off! We went lickety-split–as my dad would say any time we went fast. When we got to the bottom of the hill, we raced back up to the top to do it all over again. We laughed and laughed. Back then, it was so easy being with Daddy. We always had fun, and I felt so loved during those early years.

One evening, Mom was folding clothes, and I was ironing in our TV/music room. We were talking about an upcoming junior high dance that my parents were to chaperone.

"You know, you are your dad's favorite," my mom said, completely out of the blue.

"Why do you think that?" I asked.

"He enjoys doing things with you, and you're always game for whatever adventure he has in mind. You light up a room, and you've stopped whining!" my mom said.

We both laughed.

Actually, I thought Marcia was Dad's favorite. She was so smart and responsible, and she did what she was told more than I did.

Though this news was unexpected, I thought it was kind of neat. And I also felt a responsibility to keep the title.

Growing up, Dad taught me how to swim, ride a bike, whistle, blow bubbles with bubble gum, and drive a car. Those were my major accomplishments through my teen years! That list makes me think that maybe I shouldn't have been so surprised that I was his favorite.

However, when puberty set in, things changed. I'm sure that I wasn't moody or anything like that! Dad didn't relate to me in the same way. He became a lot stricter. I wasn't allowed to go out in cars with boys until I was 15, and my parents were strict about curfews.

Fortunately, I was allowed to have friends over, and we had parent-supervised parties that were lots of fun. Sleep-overs, too!

Dad hated all the giggling and thought we were silly, as in inane. Any time my friends were over, he sequestered himself in my parents bedroom and watched TV for the entire time. He no longer asked me to golf with him, nor did he want to come swimming with me. I imagine that he was being a busy dad to my younger brothers! He seemed detached from me. It was as if he didn't know how to talk with me anymore.

Meanwhile, at the dance, ironically, my dad still found opportunities to be playful with me. I felt proud that my parents cared enough to chaperone. Sometimes Dad would find me and grab my hand to dance. He was a really good dancer, and when we were on the dance floor, I felt lucky that he was my dad. Then, just for fun, he would dance a fast dance but get a really bored look on his face, imitating us while we danced. That embarrassed me a little.

"OH, DAD!" I'd say, with a "don't-act-so-silly-in-front-of-my-friends" look and roll my eyes.

But, my friends thought my dad was neat and that it was funny that he made fun of us! Looking back now, I can see that he *was* neat.

When my daughter, Jessica, was little, my dad seemed to think it was his job to teach her manners and good posture and to school her any lessons that I may have omitted in raising her. He also often judged what and how much she was eating. Mother was part of that as well.

The following event was a turning point in my relationship with my dad. Jessica and I were considerably overweight at various times in our lives. I recall one time when Jessica was about nine years old, and we were visiting family in Pittsburgh. We'd brought one of her friends with us and were staying in a motel that had a pool. Her friend was thin and Jessica's was chubby. We all loved to swim.

Dad came over to sit poolside and visit with me while the girls were playing in the pool. Jessica got out, walked to the deep end of the pool, shouted, "Watch me," and jumped in. Dad made this sound, "Ick," as if repulsed and shook his head. I knew immediately that he was reacting to her appearance, which was very different from her friend's.

She didn't hear him or see him shake his head, but she had antenna that would be able to sense he was repulsed by her when they spent any time together. My heart ached for her. Rough water.

As Jessica got older, especially in her punk-look years, I could tell Dad was uncomfortable being around her. A couple of years later, in front of Mother, he told me that he just couldn't love her.

"Oh, Bill, you don't really mean that," Mother said.

My dad said nothing. I told him that it broke my heart. Rough water.

Our relationship deteriorated after that. Even though my dad seemed proud of what I'd accomplished with my career at Westinghouse, he would find subtle ways to undermine my success. Every time I got a promotion and/or raise, Dad always seemed a bit jealous or resentful. Dad would say how pissed he was that I—after working for the company for just a few years—was making as much as he was after working 20 years in contracts management for Westinghouse in Pittsburgh, Pennsylvania. It was as if he was in competition with me, and I was really uncomfortable with that. Yet, even though my dad didn't tell me directly he was proud of me, I sometimes overheard him telling other people. In a way, that was hurtful, too. But at least I knew on some level he was proud. On one of his business trips to Washington, D.C. in the 1960s, he bought me a t-shirt that said, "Women belong in the house—and in the Senate."

After one of my promotions, Dad sent me a card that said "Congratulations" on the front with a picture of a professional woman in a business suit, carrying a briefcase. When you opened it up, there was a picture of the woman lying face down on the floor, with the words, "I hope it doesn't hurt too much when you fall on your face." Rough water.

In 1962, my dad lost his job and his salary was cut in half. It took an emotional toll on him. My Mother always let people know that it was then her job to build him up. And she would talk about how successful she had been with that. I'm not sure that my Dad ever lost his insecurity about losing his job.

Fortunately at that time in my life, my self-confidence was intact. I got a lot of kudos from my work. I was more interested in my boss's approval than in my Dad's. No matter how I felt undermined by my Dad's comments and actions, I was proud of what I'd accomplished as a trail-blazer for women in my career with a Fortune 100 company. And he always had a negative comment about my weight, which always infuriated me. It was not a happy father/daughter time. Unexpectedly, something changed that.

In the 1980s, Dad had been showing early signs of dementia. I remember one time, he was driving Mom to a Pittsburgh Symphony concert. He knew the route like the back of his hand. Yet, Mom told me that he pulled over on one of the streets and started to cry.

"I don't know where I am. I don't know where to go," my dad said.

But something unexpected happened. As my dad's dementia progressed, he became sweeter, funnier, less inse-cure, and kinder to me. Some special moments, music, and humor got me through those last couple of years.

This was one of those moments. When Dad was in his early 80s, he needed to have a hip replacement repair of an old hip replacement. The doctor convinced him that's what he needed. Well, it really wasn't. The second replacement went badly, and now my dad was wheelchair-bound and in extreme pain. To make matters worse, he had a torn rotator cuff and was in excruciating pain with that, too. Besides suffering from dementia, he was also depressed at that time. Things were quite bleak for him.

One day, I was visiting my dad at the nursing home where he lived and took him to his physical therapy appointment. We were sitting in the physical therapy room until his turn, and he was sighing and moaning a bit.

"Dad, are you okay?" I asked.

Dad didn't talk very much anymore, but he said, "I can't figure out how many transformers they manufacture here in this factory."

Well, if you've been around anyone with dementia, you probably know things go best if you go along with them in their world.

"Why don't you guess how many transformers they manufacture here," I said.

My dad looked at me as if I was nuts.

"I don't know, and I don't know how many trombones they make here either," my dad said. Then he looked at me with that twinkle in his eyes and continued, "But they manufacture 110 cornets." Then he immediately broke into the song, "Seventy-six trombones led the big parade ..."

And I joined in with, "... and 110 cornets close at hand."

We laughed and laughed! Other residents joined in with us, and we all laughed and sang together!

I still tear up when I think of that moment. We left a trail of Light in the physical therapy room that day!

Dad was the perfect dad when I was young and then again when he was old. Most of us have both pleasant and painful memories from our growing up and adult years. If we hold on to the pain, we never can find joy. I shed some tears writing this chapter. Thanks to therapy, I've let go of the pain and forgiven my father.

Let's hold each other in the Light as we treasure the moments that brought and bring us joy.

3

SIBLINGS

First off, let me say that I love my siblings dearly, and they all love me. Birth order: Marcia, me, Bill, and Steve. All my siblings are professed Christians–in the John 3:16 meaning of the word–and I'm an agnostic.

Some days I believe in God or a higher power, but other days, I'm just not sure. When I "pray," I hold people in the Light–a concept borrowed from the Quakers. I actually close my eyes and imagine that person (or place) bathed in light.

I believe in divine order and that all living things are part of the interconnected web of life–an idea borrowed from the Unitarian Universalists' Eight Principles. I also embrace certain qualities of the Buddhist faith, for example, that peace begins with me. Without peace in our hearts, there can be no world peace.

All that said, I think my siblings pray for me and hope that I will be "saved" one day. I don't see that happening, but they love me anyway.

One of my favorite Christian cousins, Bud Folsom, once said to me that I would make a great Christian. I was amused by that. I believe that Jesus was a remarkable man and teacher, and I hope that I lead my life in a Jesus-like manner. My sister believes that I am godlike insofar as I love unconditionally. I confess that really isn't so 100 percent of the time. But I try.

My siblings and I are very different from each other. One major difference among us is that I'm the only extravert. I married two introverts, and I think my siblings each married extroverts. I think that's interesting.

One way that we were all similar was that we played musical instruments and sang. Marcia played the flute, piccolo, and piano and sang soprano. I played the clarinet, oboe, and piano and sang second soprano or alto. Bill played trombone and sang bass. And Steve played my clarinet and sang baritone. With our parents, all six of us sang together in harmony. We learned to sing harmony very young. Actually, I don't think we needed to learn. I think that talent was inborn. We just found the sounds that fit nicely with the melody, and we sang those!

We were all smart, but Marcia and Steve stood out as being extremely bright. Marcia took calculus and passed. Steve was building his own Tandy computer when he was 13 years old.

I believe that Bill might have had some learning disabilities that the teachers nor my parents knew anything about. He did really well in some subjects but not so well in others. I was the same as far as subjects were concerned. Sometimes our parents were disappointed with Bill's and my school performances, like when our grades weren't up to snuff or when I got a D in ninth grade science. Mom and Dad were horrified. I told them it was because I leaned back in the chair and fell backward and disrupted the class. Mr. Arden said that would affect my grade.

It was true that I made a ruckus, but I'm sure it didn't affect my grade. I just didn't "get" science or math. And I had trouble with anything I had to read, such as history. I had comprehension issues due to being distracted, and I often had to reread most paragraphs a couple of times to understand them. I'm convinced that I had ADHD. I was, and still am, distracted by everything around me, including particles of dust—or dead skin–floating in the air. I was also the type of child who got "unsatisfactories" for talking too much.

My study habits changed dramatically when Robin Crossley McKelvey came to live with us for my junior year. She was an American Field Service foreign exchange student from New Zealand. We were her host family and had "adopted" her as another daughter/sister.

We lucked out! Robin knew how to study and do her homework right after she got home from school. She set an example for me, and I admired and respected her self-discipline because I had hardly any. I turned myself around, thanks to her and being on speed for weight loss!. I applied myself and completed my junior year of high school with almost all As and a couple of Bs, even in chemistry! My senior year, I did so well that I was inducted into the National Honor Society and graduated 10th in my class. In mine and Mom and Dad's eyes, I was finally "enough.'"

I loved when we did things as a family. I have many fond memories of camping, singing, playing games like charades or Tripoley, going on picnics, swimming, celebrating Christmas, going to Star Island, visiting my wonderful grandparents in Nebraska, listening to *People Are Funny* with Art Linkletter on the radio, and enjoying our traditional Sunday night dinner of popcorn, apples, and cheese. So many fun times.

One of the best experiences we had as a family was participating in a church drama, a one-act opera, *Noye's Fludde* by Benjamin Britten. Mother directed, Ed Lilley was the voice of God, Dad played Noye, I played his drunken fun-loving wife, brother Steve was the stage manager and in charge of sound and visual effects, brother Bill played the elephant, and his wife, Nancy, was one of my drunken friends. Marcia was an audience member. She lived in Charlotte, North Carolina, at the time, so she wasn't able to attend the rehearsals for the opera.

Marcia

In my eyes, my sister, Marcia, was perfect. She was 2 1/2 years older than I, and I thought that she knew everything. She remained clean, while I got dirty. She remained shod, while I lost my shoes. She knew how to tie her shoes, while I still needed help. She remained calm, while I was fidgety. She didn't wander off, while I wandered off everywhere.

The only trouble Marcia seemed to get in was when she didn't want to eat certain foods. Then she would become stubborn. Or, we would both get into trouble when we fought with each other. I fought with brute force because I was heavier and stronger than she was. She was crafty and would bite and spit. We would both kick each other while lying on our backs.

When Mom had lost all of her patience with our physical fighting, she would yell, "NO BITING OR SPITTING OR KICKING, OR ONE OF YOU IS GOING TO END UP IN TEARS!" One of us would always end up crying and run to Mom, telling how we were victimized by the other, hoping for sympathy. She wouldn't have any of it. As I look back, I don't think that Billy and Steve fought with each other like that.

When Marcia was around 14½ and I was 12, she entered a phase in which she wouldn't acknowledge me. If she saw me at school or on the way walking home, she pretended not to know me.

I was a social butterfly and somewhat popular. Marcia had one or two best friends. I had a dozen. I was a people-pleaser. Marcia didn't care what others thought of her—except maybe our parents, her teachers, and her boyfriend, Mark. I wore my hair in spit curls. Marcia wore hers in a severe ponytail. I wore corrective shoes and hated them. Marcia always had cute shoes. Mom and Dad convinced me that I needed to wear corrective shoes because my knock-knees would prevent me from being a model. Not that I ever wanted to become one!

When I was in seventh grade, Marcia got eyeglasses. I was so jealous that I faked my eye test so that I would also have glasses. Funny thing was my glasses really did help me see the blackboard better! Who knew?

Then Marcia got braces. I thought that I needed them, too, but that wasn't going to happen because I didn't have problems with the position of my teeth. One day, I stole a couple of those tiny rubber bands from Marcia, put them around my two front teeth, and told all my friends at school that the dentist was trying something new with just a few patients. I felt so much more important with those rubber bands around my teeth. That lasted about two days.

Then Marcia broke her leg and had to wear a cast and walk with crutches. She got lots of attention. I was jealous of that, but I wasn't willing to break my leg to be more like her!

The summer that Robin lived with us, we had a blast on a family camping trip to Bass Lake, Canada. Marcia was 17, Robin was 16, and I was 15.

The seven of us were packed to the gills in our 1959 Chevy two-tone tan station wagon. Once we settled into our camping spot, Marcia, Robin, and I went exploring. We met up with three really cute 20-something park rangers. All three of us flirted with those three hunks. We laughed a lot with them. We actually thought we'd picked them up! They wanted to take us out, and we were game! They decided that a drive-in movie would be fun.

We knew that persuading our parents to allow us to go was going to be tricky because they didn't know these guys. They finally gave in, I think because Marcia convinced them that she would be the chaperone! Ha!

The park rangers had two cars among them, one a Model T. Marcia and I rode in one car, and Robin went in the other. It's blurry what happened the rest of the evening, but I suspect there might have been some necking. I don't have any memory of the movie.

That was the first time Marcia and I had that kind of fun together in many years. I treasure the memory of that trip for that reason alone.

One other vivid experience from that trip was the day

and night it poured. Rather than sleep in our tents (Dad didn't want our tents to be wet for the rest of the trip!), we found a pavilion, and we all slept on picnic tables that night. We had a good laugh about that!

Years later, when Marcia was getting married, she asked me to be her maid of honor. I felt honored. Once Marcia became a wife and mother, we became much closer. Through the years, we bonded and compared notes about growing up with Mother and Dad. We would imitate our mother and laugh at our imitations!

We both had goals of not making the same mistakes as our parents had made. But at the same time, we gave them credit for doing certain things right. Marcia asked my forgiveness for treating me so badly, and I gladly did.

Then when I was planning my own wedding, I asked Marcia to be my matron of honor. She was honored as well.

Marcia is a retired tour guide at Old Salem, North Caroline, flute and piano teacher, and choir director. Her faith sustains her.

Today, Marcia is my best friend. She is one of my touchstones.

Bill

In preparation for my becoming a seven-year-old big sister, Mommy told me to come upstairs with her, that she wanted to talk with me. She took me into her bedroom, sat in her rocking chair, and asked me to come sit on her lap.

What?! I was a chubby seven year old and tall for my age as well!

I did get in her lap, and she held me so I wouldn't slide off. She didn't have much of a lap because the baby was inside her tummy. She started rocking me.

"We want you to know that after this baby is born, you will still be our dimpled darling," she said.

She hugged me and kept rocking for a little while. Looking back, that was one of the sweetest moments I ever had with my mother.

"Okay," I said and jumped off her lap to go play outside.

Billy was the most precious, sweetest baby I'd ever seen, and he was my very own brother! For the first few months after Billy was born, I became his second mother. I fed him, changed his diaper, played with him, and loved him like nothing else in the world. In all the photos that were taken in the next eight years or so, I was either holding Billy or looking at him. Up to that point, he was the best thing that happened to our family.

I never felt jealous of him, even when we sang the traditional "Hang Up the Baby's Stocking" song to him at Christmas time. That song had been sung to *me* for seven Christmases. But for Billy's first Christmas, it was sung for him, and that time I joined in the singing!

One day when Billy was around six months old, I was downstairs and heard Billy squealing at the top of our very steep, treaded stairs to the second floor. Mommy was upstairs hurrying after him, but she couldn't get to him in time. I ran to the bottom of the stairs to see Billy tumble head over heels down the steps. It was the most terrifying sight I'd ever seen. I immediately picked Billy up while he was wailing as Mommy was coming down the stairs. There were tread marks on his head. I felt terrible that I hadn't saved him from that trauma. Billy and I were both crying.

Mommy took Billy and checked him over for broken bones. She seemed to think he was okay, because she didn't call the doctor or Daddy to come take him to the ER. It's only after I became a mother that I realized how guilty Mother must have felt that she'd not been able to get to him in time.

In the summer of 1955, we went to Denver for a great family reunion with my dad's siblings and our cousins. We did so many fun things on that trip! We visited Tiny Town miniature village; saw my first Gilbert & Sullivan opera, *The Mikado*; went to Estes Park, a classic mountain village with a long heritage that is beloved for its majestic mountain beauty and free-roaming wildlife; and bonded with my cousins! We made many great memories there. Afterward, we headed back home to Pennsylvania, where we lived at the time in the Sharon-Mercer Road house.

We'd only been home for a few days when Billy, who was four years old at the time, became very sick with a high fever, flu-like symptoms, and the sudden inability to walk.

Mom and Dad quickly got a babysitter for Marcia and me, and then they rushed Billy to the ER at Sharon General Hospital. We were heartsick worrying about him. Billy was admitted to the hospital, and Mother and Dad stayed with him until visiting hours were over and then came home.

They had Marcia and me sit down in the kitchen and told us that he was diagnosed with polio and was paralyzed. We all cried.

A few minutes later, Mother called our minister from the First Presbyterian Church of Sharon to ask him to visit. He came right away. We all sat around the kitchen table while he prayed for Billy. I wanted to believe that God would hear his prayers and heal Billy.

The next day, we all went to the hospital. At that time, children weren't allowed to visit hospital patients, so Marcia and I had to wait in the car in the parking lot. Dad had parked strategically near Billy's window, which was on the third floor. Ten minutes after Dad left us in the car, he appeared in the window, holding Billy, who was smiling and waving but looking very peaked. We waved back and blew him kisses. Billy blew us kisses back.

While Billy was in the hospital, he started walking again. Dad gave him a few pennies for being such a brave little boy. Billy proceeded to put one in his mouth and accidentally swallowed it. The nursing staff had to wait for him to poop it out. We thought that it was pretty funny that someone would have to check Billy's poop for the penny! The next day it happened, and everyone was relieved.

By then, Billy's diagnosis was mild, nonparalytic poliomyelitis. We all breathed a sigh of relief. The virus affected Billy's shoulder and upper arm, and he required physical therapy to strengthen them.

In the meantime, all of us in the family needed to get gamma globulin shots to prevent us from getting polio, too. Billy was in the hospital for about two weeks, if I recall correctly. I couldn't wait for Billy to come home. I missed him terribly.

When Mom told me that I could help Billy with his physical therapy, I was ecstatic! For weeks, I worked with Billy. He was a trooper and worked really hard with his exercises. It was one of those precious times with him that I will never forget.

Here's a really funny story about bro Bill. When Marcia and I did imitations of our mother, Bill said, "I can do an imitation of Mom, too! You know those rubber tube-like girdles that Mom used to wear?" Marcia and I had no idea what was coming. "Well, this is the sound of a fart coming from inside that girdle." He held both his hands up to his mouth and made a muffled fart sound.

We all howled! Every time we're together as adults, we ask him to do that! We roll on the floor every time!

I still feel a special bond with Bill and also protective toward him. It's interesting that bro Bill feels very protective of Marcia and me even though he's our "little" brother. It's nice that he feels that way!

All four of us were wounded by our parents to varying degrees, but I believe that Bill, Steve, and I felt the wounds slightly more than Marcia. I may be wrong about that.

Bill is a wonderful Pop Pop to his granddaughter, Maggie. He works part time for a water company, and does voice work as well. When I hold Bill in the Light, I ask that he knows that he is enough.

Steve

There are 11 years between Steve and me. Steve was another precious brother. I had two sweet souls for my brothers, and I enjoyed watching them grow up.

My memories of Steve growing up are less vivid than those of Marcia and Bill. When Steve was young, I imagine

I was becoming more self-absorbed and growing into myself.

Mom and Dad were more relaxed parents with Steve than they were with Marcia, Bill, and me. I remember when I was a new mother, fretting over difficulty breastfeeding Jessica and dealing with her being a colicky baby, Dad told me, "By the time Steve came along, we simply propped the bottle up for him and left him in his crib to fall asleep." I was horrified and felt sorry that Steve might not have had the bonding that the rest of us did.

Growing up, my bedroom was next to Steve's nursery. I'd hear him wake up in the morning as I'd be getting ready to go to school. He'd play quietly with his toys, babbling happily. He never seemed to be fussy in the mornings! I'd sometimes go in to say goodbye, and he'd smile and wave. One morning, I heard him babbling, and then he said, "Mommy!" then louder, "MOMMY!"

I ran into his room, and there in the bed with him was our cat, who'd decided to have her litter of kittens in his crib! Steve was thrilled about this and clapped his hands!

Another day, I went for a walk up a hill near our house with Dad and Steve in his stroller. My dad let me push the stroller. A part of me loved doing this with my dad and youngest brother, but then I had a horrible thought, "What if someone thinks this is my baby?" I was about 13 years old, but I looked about 18. Looking back, it makes me sad to think that I was concerned about what strangers thought. At age 13, I was concerned about what *anyone* thought.

Both Billy and Steve were cute, polite kids. They shared the bedroom on the third floor of our house on East Market Street, in Mercer, Pennsylvania. They played cops and robbers, cowboys and Indians, and baseball with the

McKelvey kids next door. I'm sure they collected baseball cards because I remember them chewing bubble gum a lot!

When Steve became interested in girls, he came to me and asked me for a lesson in how to be more popular and dance. I liked that he asked me, but I'm not sure how that turned out for him. He didn't come back for lesson two. I either did a great job with the first lesson, or my teaching methods were pretty bad, and he decided to ask someone else!

We often heard from Mother and Dad that Steve was the smartest of us all, at least in math and science. We believed them. Not only had Steve built a computer, he was also a ham radio operator, and did very well in school!

"I finally got my engineer!" our dad would say, rubbing his hands together in glee.

We other three were all leaning toward careers in music. It's not that Dad was upset about that. He just really wanted a kid with a mathematical/scientific mind who could relate to him in that way. Steve was supposedly the one—until he found Christ when he was a sophomore in high school. He became very involved with an informal Christian fellowship group at school and with our church. From that point on, Steve's focus was on becoming a good Christian and giving his life to God and Christ. Steve plastered Christian posters all over his room. One birthday, I gave him a "Yield to Jesus" sign to add to the collection. He was a little embarrassed.

"You don't have to support my habit," he said.

I think I laughed!

Steve and his wife, Rhonie, became missionaries with Youth with a Mission in Amsterdam. Dad was disappointed that he lost his engineer. He felt it was a waste of a good brain.

Even though I've always loved Steve, I didn't relate to him very well–until a few years ago when he was working on his master's degree in counseling. He seemed to have opened his heart to looking at things from different perspectives and becoming less judgmental.

A few years ago, Steve called me to ask me about my memories of him growing up. I was at a loss to say much because I hadn't thought too much about him as a child other than he was really sweet and the smartest one.

In writing this, I realize that I wish I'd spent more time with Steve in his formative years like I did with Billy. It was good that he had Billy and other playmates.

As we grow older, it's a wonderful blessing that we four have each other.

4

I SURVIVED RAISING A DAUGHTER

Yes, I feel I need to repeat that: I survived raising a daughter! And she survived raising me! The journey of our mother/daughter relationship had its share of rough waters. As parents, we do our best based on what we know at the moment. Sometimes our perceptions of the moment are skewed. Let me say this, though, I am so proud of Jessica that she has worked so hard to leave trails of Light for others. She is funny, bright, sensitive, thoughtful, empathetic, industrious and generous. Here's her story.

If it weren't for the fact that I love Jessica unconditionally, I would have put her up for adoption between ages 13 and 17. Sometimes, even before those teen years, Jessica, my only child, was stubborn and willful.

At 18 months old, Jessica already had opinions about what she wanted to wear. She would always choose not to wear what I'd picked out. She had no concept of what outfits matched or what socks would match what she had on. And she liked the rattiest clothes most of all. She often left for school looking like a homeless child. Hey, I wanted to raise my child to make choices.

One day when Jessica was in preschool, I was called in for a parent-teacher conference about how Jessica dressed for school. The teachers asked if we needed help buying clothes for her, and they suggested we shop at thrift stores. I'd allowed Jessica to decorate her white sneakers with flowers, etc., to encourage her creativity, and the teachers criticized me for allowing her to not respect property. The teachers even insinuated that Jessica might not respect her body, which they cautioned could have dire consequences. By the time I left the conference, I was livid.

Jessica and I made a deal that if we couldn't agree on her outfits, she wouldn't be allowed to go to daycare. And she liked going. So that worked for the clothes. I let her wear her beloved sneakers until she outgrew them though.

Jessica learned a great deal at daycare, but to my surprise and chagrin, she learned a totally different language than we spoke at home. I discovered this one day when we were in the deli department of Giant Eagle.

"MOTHER FUCKER, DAMMIT SHIT! MOTHER FUCKER DAMMIT SHIT!" Jessica said, very loudly, in a fun sort of sing-songy way!

I was horrified!

In fact, *everyone* in the deli area was horrified.

I took Jessica firmly by the shoulders and looked her straight in the eyes.

"There are bad words that we never say in public. And there are words that you never say in front of your Nana. And there are words that you only say in your bedroom when you're alone. You just said *all* those words. Do you understand what I've told you?" I said in a controlled whisper.

Jessica nodded yes.

"I didn't know those were bad words. I thought it was a song," she said with a quivering lower lip.

Other precious times with Jessica included one rainy day during a very gloomy couple of weeks in March of 1973. She was singing "Zip-a-Dee-Doo-Dah" in her crib and looking out the window. I was thinking a more appropriate song would be "It's Raining, It's Pouring" or "Rain, Rain, Go Away."

"Oh, boo. It's raining," I said.

"Yes, isn't it beautiful?" Jessica replied.

I loved that Jessica brought Light into my life that day. I was so grateful for that.

Mother's Day, when Jessica was five, she served me breakfast in bed, which consisted of a peanut butter, dill pickle, jelly, and bologna sandwich.

"Oh, shit, I'm going to have to eat this!" I thought.

And I did! And told her it was delicious!

Other good memories with Jessica include going to the beach for a few summer vacations. One summer vacation stands out as being unique. I read an article in *McCall's* about the best summer getaways for families, including a resort in the Catskills that wasn't too far away. Besides swimming and other activities for children, the article mentioned that the resort offered special dietary options. Well, Jessica and I could afford to have some special dietary choices made for us, so we decided to go for a week.

Our first meal was dinner, and the food choices were great! I chose brisket, roasted red potatoes, and fresh green beans amandine. Jessica ordered a burger. We found it interesting that everyone else at our table was from New York City. There was a dance that night. Jessica and I like to dance, so we went. All the other dancers appeared to be 60-ish married couples who had taken the same ballroom dance classes. Jessica and I were far too intimidated by that to dance, so we retired early.

The next morning at breakfast, we looked over the menu. I decided on a cheese omelet. Bacon wasn't on the menu, but our waiter had said they prepare things not shown on the menu. When I ordered my omelet with bacon, the three couples sitting at our table looked at me as if I was a criminal.

"We will not be serving bacon with your omelet," the waiter said. "Why not?" I asked innocently. "It's not kosher," the really nice lady sitting to my right said quietly.

Okay, that had something to do with Jewish dietary laws. It was starting to dawn on me what something "dietary" meant in the magazine writeup, and I blushed in embarrassment. I apologized and explained to everyone at the table how I'd come to choose this resort. They all had a good laugh and welcomed us as guests at their table! We happened to be at THE Jewish resort of the Borscht Belt, the Grossinger Catskills Resort Hotel. I think we were the only gentiles in the entire hotel. *Mazel tov!*

As I watched Jessica in her pre-teen years, I wished that she would enjoy some of the things that Marcia and I loved growing up, such as going to Girl Scout camp, YWCA camp, and church camp; being involved in a church where she would be accepted and nurtured by her peers and learn about other religions; going to school dances and football games with friends; singing in the school chorus and maybe playing flute in the band; and being in plays. Ah, the dreams we have for our children.

But instead, Jessica ended up having 10 fabulous summers at the Pennsylvania Governor's School for the Arts at Bucknell University, in Lewisburg, Pennsylvania, a two-hour drive from Allentown, where her dad was on the theater arts faculty. What an incredible experience for her for all those years. She sat in on dozens of art and theater classes, which were a great influence on her taking metal-smithing classes at Allentown's Baum School of Art.

When Jessica was 11, she took a huge dislike to David, a guy I was dating. After one particular heated argument about him, she stomped off.

"I'm going to Pittsburgh to live with my dad!" she shouted.

In retrospect, she read David better than I had! At first, I was at first hugely saddened that she wanted to leave me, and then I was really concerned that Ed might not be up to the task of being a single parent. He and I had never discussed the possibility of Jessica living with him. There were several reasons why I didn't want her to go, but I realized that if I put my foot down, she might never forgive me.

To determine what was best for Jessica, I consulted a child psychologist and an attorney about the emotional and legal ramifications. Ultimately, reluctantly, I decided to allow her to go. Rough water!

This broke my heart. I had a really difficult time with the separation, even though I knew I'd be visiting her. Jessica lived with her father in Pittsburgh for three years. Years later, she told me that she stayed longer than she should have. I agreed. However, our relationship was much better while she was with Ed. When Jessica returned, she was 14 and facing probably the most difficult time of her life.

Early on in Jessica's life, she had been brutally bullied because of her weight. The bullying peaked when she went back to school the fall after she had come back to live with me. She was persecuted at school–spit upon, pushed down stairs, called names. Her life was even threatened–numerous times.

That November, Jessica tried taking her own life. This was a huge wake-up call for her dad and me. We listened to her cry for help.

Ed came out to show his support. We agreed she needed to be taken out of school in order to be safe. The three of us met with the school principal to develop a plan.

The principal felt strongly that Jessica should stay in school, and he assured us that the school would work out the bullying problems. He was quite adamant. I asked if he could promise that Jessica would be safe if she remained in school. He hesitated.

"No, probably not," he said.

After much discussion, we ultimately told him that we were taking her out of school and that she would study at home, which she did. She quit after several months and graduated with a GED.

That was the first time Jessica can remember that we stood firm on her behalf. In talking with Jessica about this yesterday (February 6, 2022), she wept when she said that it was the first time that she felt heard and that her dad and I together advocated for her.

It saddens me to think that it took a suicide attempt to jointly advocate for her. We had no idea to what extent the bullying was. She didn't talk about it in detail, except to say she was treated badly at school. To this day, Jessica suffers from PTSD as a result of these and other traumas. Rough water.

Little did I know that during the afternoons until I came home from work and late at night while I slept, Jessica and her friends were on the third floor of our row home, doing acid and smoking pot, self-inflicting tattoos, and listening to punk rock music. I thought about that meeting with the daycare folks about Jessica's shoes that she decorated and had some moments of guilt about that.

About a year ago, I learned that she had been raped at gun point at age 16 in our house! It breaks my heart that she didn't confide in me during those years. It wasn't until 15 years later that I learned about some of Jessica's trials and escapades directly from her. Through friends of friends, Jessica had found her "tribe," a group of teenagers who shared her angst. I wasn't a part of it. Except on Friday nights.

It might be difficult to imagine that I was included in some of the fun times with Jessica's friends. On Friday evenings, I would call up to the third floor, "Who wants to sing?"

Around six kids would bounce down the steps and fall on the first floor landing in a pile. They were like a litter of puppies! The kids would gather 'round the piano, and I'd accompany them in singing familiar songs like Billy Joel's "Piano Man," then the kids would head out the door for a night on the town. Other times we sang Christmas carols or "Memory" from *Cats*. We had so much fun singing together. I think Jessica had some of her happiest moments with her friends around that piano. I'm grateful for those friends now. A few of them stood by Jessica during her darkest times over the past 35+ years.

Later Jessica was diagnosed with major depressive disorder, panic disorder, general anxiety disorder, and post-traumatic stress disorder. Over the years, she struggled with addictions, which took their toll. Rough water.

Through it all, the only thing I knew to do was to keep loving her unconditionally.

There was one time that I had to detach myself with love from her to maintain my own sanity. She understood.

Jessica is like a phoenix rising up out of the flames. I've seen her do it several times in her life. She's a survivor. She pulled out of a very dark time and flew out of that flame. A year later, Jessica had a zaftig female-type phoenix with wings tattooed on her arm, which helped remind her that she can always rise again.

In the middle of May 1999, Jessica again decided to move to Pittsburgh to be closer to her dad. That just happened to be the week the lilacs bloomed. I was sick.

Our relationship was wonderful at the time, and I knew I'd miss her terribly. Jessica's dad was showing signs of early onset dementia. She was also missing that city. I wrote "The Mother's Day Gift" on her birthday, May 15, 1999.

The Mother's Day Gift

If children were flowers, then Jessica, my only child, would be lilacs. She was born a few days after Mother's Day, when the lilacs were in full bloom. Thanks to our many hospital visitors, lilacs surrounded us. If I could put a scent to the miracle of birth, it would be the fragrance of lilacs.

Each year as Jessica grew, having lilacs in our home for her birthday week in May became a ritual for us. We had no yard to plant a bush, but there were lovely lilac bushes behind our apartment building across the alley. At dawn, I would sneak out when the dew was still on the flowers and Jessica was still sleeping. I'd hurry so no one would see me cutting the few branches that were drooping into the alley. I considered these a part of the public domain--anyone could help themselves.

Even after I bought my house and could have planted a lilac bush, I still cut alley lilacs. When Jessica reached the age that most teenagers are embarrassed about everything their parents do, she was mortified when I got caught by a man who threatened to call the police. Intimidation and embarrassment stood in my way of helping myself to lilacs for several years. I mourned their absence.

When Jessica left home to be on her own, I needed my lilac fix more than ever. Jessica knew me well, but she knew the alleys even better. Little did I know that she had been scouting them for years. Jessica is not a morning person, though, so she shifted the ritual clippings to late night, and the sins of the mother continued.

Five years ago, the ritual changed dramatically. It was Mother's Day and the lilacs were in full bloom. Jessica invited me to her apartment for the afternoon. I was certain my Mother's Day gift would be a big bouquet of lilacs that she'd cut the night before.

When I entered her apartment, in the middle of her living room, I saw the most incredibly beautiful purple lilac bush I had ever seen—blossoms, roots, and all. Several cards were tucked among the branches. I stood in the doorway and cried.

This was, by far, the most precious Mother's Day gift ever--a permanent symbol of her birth. Later that day, we planted it in a corner of my yard so that I could always see it from my kitchen window.

Jessica turns 28 today, and in a few days, she is moving 300 miles away. My enormous lilac bush is laden with blossoms. The fragrance is heady. I've not pruned the alley side of my bush so that passers-by will be able to easily help themselves to their share of my treasured gift. I carefully clip several blossoms to take inside. I bury my face in one of the blooms. I tear up. If I drink in enough of the sweet scent, I'll be able to remember the miracle of Jessica—even after she has moved and the blossoms are gone.

After Jessica had made her decision to move to Pittsburgh, she went online to find new friends who could show her around. It had been 14 years since she'd lived there, and the city had changed a lot. One of the respondents was Jake, who was planning on moving back to the Pittsburgh area as well, having just completed his degree at Louisiana State University.

For three months before Jessica and Jake both moved to Pittsburgh, they talked for hundreds of hours on the phone and chatted online. They became great friends and very soon fell in love. When they settled into Pittsburgh, they finally met face to face. To everyone's surprise, a month later, Jessica found out she was pregnant. They decided to get married. Jessica gave birth to my granddaughter, Kate Savannah Krizmanich, in February 2000. Most of us were quite concerned about the speed with which all of this happened. But, hey, it's their life. We wished them well. And we loved being grandparents!

The marriage lasted seven years.

In the 1990s, Jessica started working with people with disabilities, as both her dad and I had done. Ed and I had leadership roles at an Easter Seals Society camp for four summers. It's a field made for her skillset: a combination of compassion, industriousness, leadership, a sense of humor, and people skills.

By the time Jessica was ready to go to work after Kate was born, she had enough experience under her belt to land a great job in her field with a Pittsburgh agency. She was quickly promoted to assistant director of employment services, and she increased their referrals by 900 percent! She became known as an expert in her field statewide. In the midst of all of this, Jessica earned a bachelor of arts degree in studio arts with a second major in business from Cedar Crest College, and graduated summa cum laude! It took her 11-1/2 years to finish her degree because she worked full time while taking classes and took three years off to be with Kate. I couldn't be prouder of how she stuck with that journey.

Yet some of Jessica's darkest times were still ahead of her. Between 2015 and 2018, she lost her health, her career, and her home.

It took two years of symptoms, appointments with

several specialists, and hours of Jessica's own research to finally diagnose her with Ehlers-Danlos Syndrome, a rare genetic disorder of connective tissue. It is generally characterized by joint hypermobility, instability, and dislocations, and it affects every body system. To date, Jessica has had 10 surgeries.

Due to this debilitating, degenerative syndrome, Jessica had to fight for three years to get her disability insurance. She was unable to keep working when her life was consumed by physical therapy and doctor's appointments. Over time, Jessica lost the ability to walk, sit, or stand for more than 15 minutes at a time. She also lost joint stability in her hands. Because of this, she is limited with cooking, getting dressed, typing, folding her clothes, and doing the crafts that she loves. She lost her career, which she so loved. Her rheumatologist told her that she will be wheelchair-bound in about three years. Rough water.

Fast forward to 2016. Jessica suspected that her Morningside, Pennsylvania, house might have toxic, black mold, which she was certain she smelled. But she couldn't afford to do anything to fix it. For two years, Jessica and Kate lived there with that fear. Finally, Jessica could afford to have a professional remediation company inspect the home, and they found extensive black mold in the walls and basement of her house. Rough water for them!

Jessica, Kate, and their two dogs needed to move out ASAP! They put their house up for sale, and it sold in five days—as is! They asked Bill and me if they, meaning Jessica, Kate and their two dogs, could come live with us until they found an apartment, which they figured might take six months to a year. We supported this idea wholeheartedly, knowing that they would have been homeless otherwise. It took more than two years for the horrible symptoms they had from the black mold to be gone.

Having three generations under one roof turned out to be a joy—most of the time. 17-year-old Kate hadn't really wanted to move, and she was moody, sullen, and depressed most of the time she lived with us. She refused to take her medication, which she needed for depression and social anxiety. Kate and Jessica often fought.

Jessica was crowded in her small bedroom, and Kate slept in our three-season room, which varied in temperature from 35° to over 100°—despite heaters and air conditioners.

Jessica and I had both grown up since her teenage years, which made living with each other wonderful! Therapy had helped both of us. And Bill lived with all these females! How he maintained his sanity amidst the three of us, I'll never know. He was always the voice of reason!

Before Jessica and Kate moved in, Bill and I had been talking about moving. We couldn't afford to be homeowners anymore, and taking care of our property was becoming more work than what we were able to do or finance.

By fall 2019, Jessica and Kate had been living with us for more than two years—past even the worst-case scenario they gave when they asked us to move in. In September, we told them that our plan was to sell our house in six months or less.

We decided to put it on the market right away. We all had a shitload of work to do to whip that house into shape. In the beginning of December, we got an offer on the house, and we closed 12 days later! January 15, 2020, was the moving date for all four of us—plus two dogs and a cat.

Bill and I moved to an apartment in an Allentown suburb. Jessica and Kate moved into an apartment just 10 minutes away. It's been two years since we all moved, and I still miss them. But Bill and I have gotten used to having our own living space again.

In the next couple of months, Kate, then 20 years old, fell in love with Mike, a man from New Jersey. They became engaged and made plans to live with Mike's parents. She wanted to be with him, and Jessica let her use her wings to fly.

One year later, we were all surprised to find out that we were going to be blessed with a baby girl. Mike and Kate were also surprised, but excited about the prospects of being parents. Beautiful Jada was born on August 11, 2021. Jessica, or OoMah, as she wants to be called, has embraced the idea of being a grandmother, and Bill and I have happily taken on being Great OoMah and Great Grandpa Bill. We love having more family to love! Exciting times.

For now, Jessica's life is very difficult, but it is punctuated by moments of joy and fun. Despite the chronic pain she's in and the loneliness that she's felt during the Covid-19 pandemic, she creates moments of joy for herself and her dog, Lilley. She finds much joy in being with Jada. She recently started a part time job as an instructional aide for a young man with disabilities, and she is excited to have more meaning in her life as a result. On a good day, her hands create miniatures for her doll house and other crafts.

Jessica, I wish health and happiness for you. Thank you, my dear daughter, for all that you are. Keep leaving those trails of Light. I will love you unconditionally, always and forever.

5

BAGGAGE OVERLOAD

We all carry baggage from our childhoods, and sometimes we even *create* baggage as the years go by. "Baggage" is unresolved shit. We lug it around. It weighs us down. Sometimes, we open it up, pull out stuff, and ruminate on it. Or we just bury the whole damn suitcase and never unpack it. And then we're really fucked up.

There are two kinds of baggage: The first is happenstance baggage, what happens to you along the way, the situations that occur, environmental influences—the milieu.

The second kind is the baggage that we're born with—genetic baggage. This might include mental health issues, learning disabilities, and even genetic/hereditary disorders and diseases.

Worth

Worth - /wərTH/; *noun, the level at which someone or something deserves to be valued or rated.*

In our family, worth was based on two things: appearances and accomplishments. If you were a good citizen, a stalwart Christian, and a happy family, or *appeared to be,* you were worthy of respect and admiration. If you had a long list of accomplishments, you were worthy of respect and love from your parents. If you were smart, you were worthy. If you had good manners, you were worthy. If you helped without being asked, you were worthy. If you were thin, you were worthy. If you had a college degree, you were worthy. The list went on and on.

However, if you *failed* at any of these things, you weren't quite enough to be worthy of unconditional love.

For example, if Dad thought you were fun, then you were worthy of spending time with him doing fun things. He took me with him golfing. That was a treat. I learned how to stand still and shut up when he was getting ready to swing or putt. I got to hold the flag and keep it from waving while he putted. After the last hole, he bought us both spicy hot dogs. I still love hot dogs! When I was 10, he treated me to golf lessons in hopes that I'd play with him. I wasn't very good, and after three lessons, we stopped. I felt like a failure, and he said he was disappointed. This was the beginning of feeling that I wasn't enough and that Dad loved me less.

When I was growing up, we would play board games as a family. One of my parents' favorites was *Go to the Head of the Class.* I dreaded playing it. You would answer questions, and if you were right, you could move your "person" token up toward the head of the class based on the number on the dice roll. The person who reached the head of the class first won.

I never won.

I didn't always know the answers, unlike my parents and sister. When I would read a question, Mom would say, "You'll know this one, Mary. Everyone knows the answer to this one."

Well, I didn't, and I would give my best guess, which would be wrong.

"It isn't cute to act dumb!" Mom would say.

My eyes would well up with tears.

"But I really didn't know the answer," I'd defend myself.

"How could you not know that answer?" Mom would ask.

No one came to my defense. I wasn't enough. And if I wasn't enough, I wasn't worthy, and I perceived they wouldn't love me as much.

The Matriarch's Scripts

Matriarch - /ˈmātrēˌärk/; *noun; a woman who is the head of a family or tribe.*

PSYCHOLOGY **Script***: the social role or behavior appropriate to particular situations that an individual absorbs through cultural influences and association with others.*

Mother had scripts and expectations for almost everything. It was as if she was living in a play, and she was the script writer, director, producer, and lead actress. In her play, everyone was thin and attractive. They made their beds, brushed and flossed their teeth twice a day, ate everything on their plates, went to church, went to college, and never wore white before Memorial Day or after Labor Day. They did washing on Mondays and ironing on Tuesdays. They married an ambitious man and didn't have too many children—too many being more than four. There was no such thing as depression. People were sad from a situation that they would get over quickly. They just needed to think happy thoughts.

Mother allowed no negative emotions. She suffered from toxic positivity—"the belief that no matter how dire or difficult a situation is, people should maintain a positive mindset. It rejects difficult emotions in favor of a cheerful, often falsely positive, façade," as Kendra Cherry explains on Verywellmind.com.

It would have been inconceivable to Mother that positivity could be toxic. Her positivity often borderlined strong denial about anything negative, including emotions. She would use phrases like, "Keep your chin up." "Oh, don't feel that way. Life is too precious to be angry (or sad or depressed or resentful)." "No more tears." "No pouting." "No whining."

She liked to play the "Put on a Happy Face" game. If we were pouting, she would give us a handkerchief to hold up to our faces. Only when we were smiling were we allowed to drop it. To this day, I can still put on a happy face when my internal self might be suffering. Sometimes that's a good thing. Sometimes not.

More scripts. Her Three-Day Rule applied to the number of days we were allowed to be sick, and it also applied to overnight guests. She would always say, "Guests are like fish. They begin to smell after three days."

Mother even had scripts about grieving. She was the kind of person who might say to someone grieving, "I'm sorry for your loss, but you should count your blessings." She believed that the process of grieving should last a short amount of time. Maybe weeks! Certainly not a year. People should know that life goes on and that grieving was a waste of time.

The most tragic episode of this judgment came when bro Bill and Nancy lost their second son during childbirth. Mother was shocked when they gave the full-term fetus, as she perceived it, a name: Alan. And that they wanted a small memorial service for him along with a coffin. It was a really difficult time for Nancy and Bill, and they needed to grieve in this perfect way. They buried this precious baby on top of his grandfather, who had died suddenly when Nancy was a teenager. Understandably, Nancy and Bill still grieve that loss. Mother never understood that either.

Because I adopted many of my mother's scripts, it took years of therapy before I finally felt free from her control to accept a promotion and leave Pittsburgh and move to Allentown, Pennsylvania. It was the first of many freeing things in my life. I was evolving into being my own person, and I liked me as I was. Well, almost.

Emotional Eating

Medical definition: *Emotional eating is the practice of consuming large quantities of food—usually "comfort" or junk foods—in response to feelings instead of hunger.* Experts estimate that 75 percent of overeating is caused by emotions.

Another miscellaneous piece of baggage includes food. Both of my parents struggled at times with weight, more so Mother than Dad. She went on the Atkins original diet once and lost 80 pounds. She told people that the first thing she ate when she added some things back into her diet were parsnips. I think that she was proud that it wasn't pasta, potatoes, or candy. Those would have been too bourgeois for her. More scripts!

How many women struggle with body issues? Mine started early. I wore Chubette sized clothing until I was about 12 when Chubettes didn't accommodate boobs. I'd thinned out a bit and started wearing more fashionable clothing with my corrective shoes. In the next year or so, I started putting weight on, and Mother decided that I might do well with diet pills, which were in essence, amphetamines, a psycho-stimulant or "speed." The doctor prescribed speed during my junior and senior years of high school. Thanks to speed and Robin's influence, my grades turned around! I needed much less sleep, and I was pretty happy all the time.

Quite frankly, I loved my speed years! If I had attention deficit hyperactivity disorder (ADHD), I'm certain that my H was off the charts. I became gutsier. My junior year, I auditioned for cheerleading. I looked different from all the varsity cheerleaders. I was tall, almost 5'8", big-boned, ashy blonde, and probably 15 to 20 pounds overweight, which meant I was fat in the eyes of the judges even though I could do everything well.

I didn't make the team, so I became the high school mascot for Mercer Mustangs during my senior year for basketball season. I wore a horse costume with a papier-mâché head that was covered in soft, fake horse hair. But when I attended Grove City's senior prom with Dave, I wore a size 10, pale blue chiffon dress. Dave was in my life a couple more times. He became one of the "so many men." He came with me to my 15th high school reunion and then we dated again when I was in my late 30s.

When I went away to college, I went off speed and gained 40 pounds. Got married. Gained 30 more pounds. Got divorced. Lost 20 pounds. Started dating. Lost another 20 pounds. Took a hiatus from dating and gained 30 pounds. Started dating Bill and gained 75 pounds. See a pattern here?

I tried every diet out there over the years—even injections from pregnant womens' urine! I probably spent thousands of dollars on programs. I reached my peak weight of 300+ pounds when I was 58 years old. I had type 2 diabetes, high blood pressure, and sleep apnea. My internist gave me 15 more years to live if I kept up what I was doing. That was a wake-up call.

Two years later, *after my mother died*, I made a decision to have Roux-en-Y gastric bypass surgery. I had surgery the day before my 60th birthday. I still think it's really interesting that I waited until my mother died to become "thin." It was almost as if I wouldn't give her the satisfaction of thinking that she had anything to do with it. Pretty self-defeating and dysfunctional thinking, huh?

I lost 120 pounds, and I was happy in my size 12 to 14

pants and medium-large tops. I maintained that weight loss for 16 years, plus or minus 15 pounds. It's an ongoing process, but I'm ever so grateful that I lost all that weight finally. My doctor's office says I'm their poster child for success with gastric bypass. Yay!

The Covid 19 pandemic added 20 pounds to my body! I panicked a little bit with that and had some trouble taking it off, so I joined WW (formerly Weight Watchers). I took off the 20 pounds s-l-o-w-l-y. I'm still about 25 pounds over-weight, so I'm going to stick with WW to take it off.

All my siblings have struggled with weight, too. We have a history of thinking that food is equated with love and caring or that it was a reward for something. Food was comfort that soothed the soul. It was a drug that became an addiction for Marcia and me. Back in the late 1970s, we joined Overeaters Anonymous. We learned a lot about our compulsions and obsessions with food, and we bonded even more as sisters and friends. I'm still capable of overeating and being compulsive about food, but I've learned portion control, which I practice 80 percent of the time. It works.

Genetic Baggage

Depression, Anxiety, and Bipolar Disorder

I have major depressive disorder, general anxiety disor-der, and certain behaviors of bipolar disorder. I don't feel shame or embarrassment about any of that. Call me crazy!? No! I have chemical imbalances in my brain. I say this because I'm anxious for the negative stigma about mental illness to just go away. I think having a sense of humor about it helps me share with others.

These are diagnoses from my qualified psychiatrist, Stephen, and therapist, Harold, who has a PhD in psychology, and an MSW (masters in social work). I diagnosed myself with ADHD because I took an online quiz and scored really high! I have mental illnesses, but most folks would think I am fairly grounded and happy. That's because I've worked hard on my behaviors and dramatic emotional swings. I'm also on Cymbalta and Abilify, which work really well. And I've learned that I don't always have to put on a happy face! I'm blessed.

Unfortunately, many folks with mental illness go untreated, don't want to take their meds, or can't find the right meds. Or they're ashamed that they can't just get over their feeling sad or "nervous." Therapy and meds have been lifelines for me, and I actually "graduated" from therapy several months ago! Yeah, I know. I didn't know that was possible.

I've had some major health issues that affected my sanity. Here's one example: In 2010, I was rushed to the hospital via ambulance with symptoms that included a high fever from an infection and the inability to form sentences and speak coherently. The doctors tested me for stroke, which turned out to be negative, but the MRI showed three unruptured brain aneurysms! WTF!? Bill and I followed up with the chief of neurosurgery at our regional health center. I wanted nothing but the best, and he was considered the best.

Dr. Li told Bill and me that the largest aneurysm could be clipped, which would require a craniotomy! WTF?! And he said that the smaller aneurysm would require coiling via interventional radiology surgery.

Dr. Li explained the risks of the craniotomy—hey, we're talkin' brain surgery risks—which included stroke, coma, and even death. Rough water. I was numb.

The largest aneurysm was located in the speech part of my brain, so there was also a risk of losing my speech. I was even more numb. I couldn't talk. I felt a panic attack coming on. I wanted to go home, go to bed, and not think about any of it. More rough water.

"I think Mary has a lot to think about. We'll get back to you in a day or so," Bill said.

And we left. On the way home, as Bill was wont to do, he decided he would make a spreadsheet the next day showing the odds of the risks between having surgery and not having surgery. He spoke in ratios and percentages, and I felt I might throw up. I told him this wasn't helping and to just be quiet. Poor guy. This was hard for him, too.

I became more despondent and depressed about the thought of becoming an invalid or losing my speech. For God's sake, I was a professional speaker with a full-time job for which I needed to use my voice daily. I didn't want to become a burden on Bill or Jessica. I was ridden with anxiety, and I felt desperate and hopeless.

A day later, I was on my way home from work and figured I had a solution. I would drive my car into a brick building going 55 mph. I would die on impact. It would be over. I was serious. I came home and cried. I didn't really want to die, but I couldn't face the alternatives if the surgery didn't go well.

That night I became very quiet, which is always a sign of depression for me. I finally told Bill that I couldn't go through with the surgeries. The risks were way too over-whelming. I blurted out that I felt like driving into a brick wall and ending this anxiety and depression. He was horrified. He said he thought I again needed help from Harold. He convinced me to call him, and I felt some relief when I heard his voice. I asked if I could see him NOW. Bill drove me to Harold's office because I was a mess.

Harold helped me change my mind about suicide during that hour that I cried. I saw him twice a week for several weeks. My family prayed for me to heal. They didn't know about my ideation at the time. Bill was the perfect husband for me through that time. Therapy helped me make the decision to have both brain surgeries.

Three months later, I was at total peace with the thought of the craniotomy I was about to have. It was successful, and I still had my speech, although I still sometimes have trouble retrieving words and a malapropism will pop out of my mouth on occasion. Or sometimes aphasia. I just laugh, knowing it could have been so much worse.

Humor has gotten me through many difficult times in my life—as have possibly my siblings' prayers! But more than anyone, Bill was my lifeline back to sanity. Without him, I'm not sure I would have made it.

Mental illness was definitely a part of our family. As Dad aged, he showed signs of early dementia (forgetfulness) and depression. Mother was in complete denial of this. She would give him tests: "What did we have for breakfast?" "What movie did we watch last night?" When he couldn't remember, she would tell him if he only tried harder he would, with impatience and disgust in her voice. Dad would feel terrible and withdraw. He felt bad enough not being able to remember and mother never got that. If he was withdrawn and sullen, she would say, "Oh, Bill, all you have to do is think happy thoughts." "Oh, get over it, Bill. Don't be so sad. There's nothing to be sad about." "Put on a happy face." She said all of these things in varying forms to all of us.

Later on, Dad was diagnosed with clinical depression. Mother was shocked, but at the same time she started to realize that Dad wasn't just sad. She seemed to slowly accept that he wouldn't get over it in three days! He was put on medication, which helped a little. Unfortunately, this didn't help Mother in knowing how to be with him. She was more impatient with him than ever.

Dad's dementia became worse, and he was diagnosed with Alzheimer's disease by his primary care provider. Years later, after receiving in-depth training in Alzheimer's disease and dementia while working at a continuous care retirement community, I believed that he had vascular dementia, which is quite different from Alzheimer's disease.

Dad became more confused, but also became funnier and sweeter. I think he was happier–freed from guilt and inadequacy. He was actually nicer to me.

As my dad's dementia progressed, Mother never enjoyed visiting with him. She didn't know how to interact with him. She would start every sentence with, "Bill, do you remember the time when we …?" Of course, he couldn't. But he still loved music, and he would often sing with people, remembering most of the words.

When Mother and Dad were in their early 80s, they realized they could no longer live in their home. Dad had fallen several times, and Mother couldn't care for him anymore. They moved to an independent living facility.

Even after they moved, they weren't safe. My dad kept

falling, and Mother was in a tragic accident while riding in the facility's van. She wasn't completely buckled in, and the van was hit by a tractor trailer. Mother went flying and shattered her left leg. She was no longer able to walk, and she had become totally blind from macular degeneration and diabetic retinopathy. Mother was moved to assisted living while Dad was in the secured dementia unit.

One day, Bill and Nancy decided to take Dad for a visit to Mother's apartment. When they arrived, Dad, a man of few words by this time, looked at Mother.

Now THAT'S a piece of baloney!" he said.

We all laugh every time Bill and Nancy tell that story!

Depression runs in our family. Besides Dad, all four of us siblings have been on medication for depression at one time or another. Certainly one of the reasons might be genetic, but I wonder how much had to do with living in a judgmental and conditional love environment while growing up. My depression was certainly made more complex by feeling I wasn't enough. Through therapy, Cymbalta, and Abilify, I've been able to manage my depression and anxiety quite well. And I have moments of joy and gratitude about my life. And I am enough! Yay and hallelujah!

PART II

SO MANY MEN, SO LITTLE TIME

"I thought I was promiscuous, but it turns out I was just thorough."
—**Russell Brand**

6

THE BEGINNING

When I was in junior high school, I had crushes on about 11 guys in my class. Of those 11, I think I only went on one date with one of them—Bill, and on several dates with Franz. I wanted to go out with John, Carl, Alan, Hank, Will, Paul, Bob, Bob, and Bob.. I think that John was the only one who knew about my crush. I flirted pretty openly with him. And I didn't talk about my list with any of my friends. So many boys—so much time.

I still have kind of a crush on one of the Bobs. Actually, our relationship is more like best friends who act goofy together. Bob is a whole lot of fun and can make me laugh. We also can talk about any personal subjects. We had a casual date when we were in our late teens, after we'd been in college a year. I kind of screwed up any possibility of our dating seriously because I laughed when he tried to kiss me. I was insecure and a bit taken back and nervous, and I thought he was kidding, so I laughed. He felt rejected. I'm sorry, Bob. I love you, and I treasure our goofy lifetime friendship.

My sophomore and junior years consisted of guys who played in the Grove City High School band. We'd met them at the snack bar after the half-time show and became great friends. There was James, Terry, and Ben, who were best friends. I dated Ben first. He was a super guy. We double dated with James and his girlfriend, Carol. Terry and a girl named Susan dated. Ben and I broke up–can't remember why. Then I dated James for a while. I introduced Ben to one of my best friends, Sarah, and they went steady for a while. They were like this perfect couple. Lots of good times! I learned how to kiss really well thanks to the Grove City guys, and later, my classmate, Bill, reaped the benefit. At our 40th high school reunion, he told me it was the best kiss he'd ever had in his life. He said this in front of his wife, whom he adored. I felt a bit embarrassed and a little proud.

My senior year, I ended up going steady with Jeff, who was a year behind me and his class's clown. We had fun together. At least I did. We'd have a date, then go parking, and I finally allowed him to touch me below my neck, which was about 1/2 inch below my collarbone. He knew he could turn me on by touching me that close to my boobs. I'd get breathing pretty heavily then say, "Okay, I can't do this anymore!"

He was always respectful of me, which I really appreciated at the time. He got other "feels" while we horsed around at Brandy Springs swimming pool. He'd grab me from behind around my waist and lift me up and down, dunking me, and every once in a while he'd accidentally touch my boob or my butt. At the time, I just thought we were two kids playing in the water. I was so naïve!

I happened to see him when I came home after my first year in college. He assumed that I had gotten completely educated while there and suggested that we do "it." I laughed and said that I was still a virgin and planned on staying that way until I was married. He was disappointed and slightly shocked. He still has my class ring. Jeff, may I have it back?

At the University of Nebraska, I was perceived as the sophisticated big city easterner, even though I lived in Mercer, Pennsylvania, which at the time had a population of about 3,400. In the eyes of a midwesterner, we were in close proximity to the big city of Pittsburgh. I had joined a sorority, Alpha Chi Omega. I'd recently been voted my pledge class's president, and I was considered a fun date. However, many guys didn't ask for a second date because I didn't "put out." That was okay, because there were so many men!

My two favorite U of N guys were Ken, a football player and John, a Sigma Chi.

Soon the tides would change.

7

FIRST LOVE

It was the summer of 1962. We lived in Sherwood Forest.

I had just completed my freshman year at the University of Nebraska. The other counselors and I wore cut-off jeans and unbleached duck cloth, hooded shirts over the cutoffs. We thought we were very cool, and of course, we assumed others thought the same.

I was nicknamed "Little John" because I was the tallest, biggest-boned unit counselor. "Robin" was our unit leader—a bit roly-poly, delightful, and competent. She could be silly but not as crazy fun as "Friar Tuck," "Maid Marian," and I were!

I was the assistant unit leader, considered the Amazon woman of the pack, competent, and a bit crazy—in a good way. Friar Tuck was fun, but not very competent. Maid Marian took orders well.

We four counselors lived in a three-sided shack, and we slept on straw tick mattresses on squeaky, rusty cots. We didn't mind. We were so exhausted by the time we went to bed that no one cared how uncomfortable they were!

The camp was located in a valley in which the air didn't move much, thus everything was damp, dank, and fermented-smelling. But the smell of the pines permeated everything. I loved that smell.

Most nights, after we had tucked all the little Girl Scout campers in for the night, the other counselors and I ceremoniously burned sandalwood incense and lit vanilla scented candles. With these scents as a backdrop, we sang songs like "Where Have All the Flowers Gone," "Dona, Dona," and "Kumbaya." I accompanied on the guitar.

We got pretty creative with our talents, and we used them for barter because we were all poor! One night, I ran out of cigarettes, and Maid Marian needed a haircut. I got my scissors out and offered to barter a trim for a pack of smokes. She agreed, and so we did. There's nothing like the barter system! I'd kept myself supplied in cigarettes by cutting hair in college.

After a fun summer, I returned to U of N for my sophomore year. I majored in a social life!

I think I dated 12 guys that year—until I met Josh. I thought I was in love, and we necked and danced to Johnny Mathis songs in the basement of his fraternity house.

I was smitten with Josh. He was a Sigma Alpha Mu, who were more popularly known as Sammies. It was a Jewish fraternity, and I'd never met a Jewish person before.

Josh was also the Cornhuskers' mascot—an ear of corn —because he was so tall, 6' 7". He and I became lavaliered, which meant we were dating exclusively. He took me to Omaha to meet his family. We broke up at the end of that year. It was maybe too serious for me. And besides there were so many men—so little time.

At U of N, my sorority sisters taught me how to play bridge, and we smoked cigarettes and ate chips while we played during lunch time. Others watched soap operas, but we thought they were stupid. The soap operas.

One night, a friend invited me to a bridge party at a friend of a friend's apartment. I went. There were eight of us there, two tables of players. The choices of drinks were water or beer. I didn't like beer. I wasn't a huge fan of water either, but I decided on a beer–just because. We were bidding a hand, I took a sip.

"Two hearts," I said. Suddenly everyone started to scramble. Guys were climbing out of the windows, and someone was grabbing all the bottles of beer and pouring them down the kitchen sink. I just sat there wondering what the hell was happening like a lost puppy. I was so naïve.

Yup! We were being raided!

The police banged on the door, and one of the guys let him in. After a brief search, the police were especially angry because they couldn't find any partially emptied bottles of beer. Five of us were taken by police cars to the police station, which smelled of mustiness, paper, and men. Three of us were charged with underaged drinking and two for influencing minors.

I called my great Aunt Ruth in tears. She got me a lawyer, who magically took care of things for me and drove me home to my dorm. His fee was $100. My parents told me I'd have to pay them back for his services as part of my punishment. And Camp Riamo, a southeastern Girl Scout Camp, hired me for $100 for the summer. Thus, Little John.

Back to camp. Camp life was fun. I met some other

great counselors, one of whom was nicknamed Happy Tooth. She talked adoringly of her English and speech teacher, Ed Lilley. She told me that I reminded her of a woman gymnast who Ed apparently was intrigued with.

"You need to meet this guy. I think you were made for each other! He's doing summer stock theater in Uniontown, playing the role of the sheriff in *A Streetcar Named Desire*," she said.

I thought, "OMG, an actor!"

I'd always been intrigued with acting, and truth be told, I'd wanted to be an actress since I was four years old. Happy Tooth called Ed from the camp office to make arrangements for several of us to come and see the play.

Three of us were able to take the night off–a rarity. We were so excited to be out at a dinner theater! The play started, and we were mesmerized. Ed was brilliant. And he had a gorgeous, baritone voice–the kind of voice that made you melt. I was already imagining co-starring in *The Music Man* with him!

After the show, Ed joined us at our table, and we talked for hours. I was taken in, mainly by the smell of the grease-paint! I held my breath in hopes that he would ask me out. We stood to leave, and I kept looking up at that giant of a man–6'4". It took a man 6'4" for me to feel non-Amazon-like. I liked it. As we left, I kind of held back, waiting for the big move!

When I was just about out the door, he asked, "Mary, may I call you? I think it would be fun to spend some time together and get to know each other."

Afraid I'd say something stupid, I said, "I guess so," which was pretty stupid. And that's all I said. And left. Of course we had no cell phones then, so how the hell was he supposed to get a hold of me? Oh, my! I thought to myself that I'd have to call him, but girls don't call guys. That was another one of my mother's scripts. I got his phone number from Happy Tooth.

Two nights later, I made the call. I was in the camp director's office with the camp director sitting there. She seemed amused by my obvious anxiety because she had this grin on her face. My hands were sweaty.

I took several deep breaths and dialed. My heart was pounding in my throat. I was looking forward to hearing Ed's voice again. A woman answered on the second ring. What? I wasn't ready for that. I paused. She said, "Hello?" She sounded older, like 50 or 60.

"Hi, is Ed there?" I said, thinking, "Damn, why didn't I say something like, 'Hi, this is Mary Hammond. I met Ed last week after his performance at the dinner theater. Is he there?'"

"Are you Mary?" the woman asked.

I was stunned. I remembered my mother's script. I shouldn't have called. It wasn't ladylike.

"Yes. Mary Hammond."

"He was hoping you might call. Hold on. I'll get him."

What? He was hoping I might call? Wait. He didn't have the same script! How could that be?

"Hello? Mary," breathing a little heavy.

"Yes, hi, Ed."

Silence. He was still out of breath.

"I'm sorry, what did I take you from? You sound out of breath."

"I was picking potatoes from my dad's garden and ran to the house. I was glad to hear you had called, especially since I didn't have a good way of contacting you."

He was glad to hear from me. Okay, this was good.

"You mentioned maybe we could get together," I said.

"I'd love that!" He sounded pretty excited about this prospect. "Do you like to dance?"

"I love to dance!" I was imagining him dipping me down at the end of a romantic dance to "The Twelfth of Never."

"Where and when? My night off is next Tuesday." OMG! I sounded way too eager.

"That will work for me. We'll pick you up at 8:30," Ed said.

Wait, did he say "We'll pick you up?" or did he say "Will pick you up?" Oh, for God's sake, he's an English and speech teacher. He said "We'll!"

"Are we going with another couple?" I asked. "You said, 'We'll.'"

Silence. Uh, oh.

"Um, this is a little awkward. I hope you understand. Um, I don't drive. My dad and I will pick you up," he said.

I thought this was a bit unusual but intriguing. Kind of refreshing. Threw me back to when I was 15, and a date's dad would pick me up!

"Sure. Yes. I mean that's fine."

"Ok then, Tuesday at 8:30 it is. I'll see you then."

"Right. Until then. Bye."

"Bye."

I breathed a sigh of relief.

"I have a date!!!" I said to the director.

"I know. I heard," she said laughing.

Happy Tooth had been waiting outside the office for me. I told her the news, and we hugged each other and danced around doing swing your partner! I ran back to my unit to tell everyone. They were all excited for me and listened with baited breath to every detail of the phone conversation. They oohed and aahed and laughed with each bit of information.

I knew exactly what I was going to wear for our date: my cotton, lime green two-piece dress—a gored skirt and Mandarin-collared jacket with an off-white braided belt that had a leather buckle. I had white sandals. Perfect. The lime green would show off my summer tan and sun-bleached hair. I packed that dress for camp at the last minute, thinking, "Where will I ever wear it?" Who knew! Do men spend time like this on their first-date outfits?

On Tuesday night, as I waited in the gravel parking lot for Ed and his dad, I wondered what Ed would be wearing. Then anxiety set in with the "what ifs." What if I didn't sound cool? What if we had nothing to talk about? What if he didn't think I was attractive? What if I thought he was weird? What if his dad didn't like me? What if he didn't like me? What if I threw up? What if I needed to go to the bathroom? What if I farted? What if I couldn't follow his dancing lead? And on and on.

Ed's dad pulled up beside me, and Ed got out of the front seat of the older model car—a Ford, I think. He looked so cool! He wore tan chinos with one of those little belts in the back that did nothing. His shirt was soft cotton in a beautiful shade of blue. He looked good in blue. Actually, I thought he'd look good in anything.

Ed introduced me to his dad, who said, "Nice to meet you, Mary."

"Nice meeting you, too, Mr. Lilley," I said, leaning into the car.

It felt stilted. We didn't shake hands. I assumed that we'd

sit in the backseat, but NOOOOO, Ed motioned for me to get in and slide over until my arm was up against his dad's arm. Then he got in, and I was smushed between these two strange men.

Mr. Lilley smelled of chewing tobacco, and I could see the shape of the wad inside his cheek. I threw up a little in my mouth.

Ed smelled of Grand Bay Lime Bay Rum aftershave, which was intoxicatingly erotic. I'd put a tiny dab of Tabu cologne behind my ears and was hoping it might have the same effect on Ed. My clothes smelled of campfire smoke, sandalwood incense smoke, and Salem cigarette smoke. I realized I was reeking up the entire car. I apologized for stinking up the car, kind of kidding. Mr. Lilley said nothing. Well, I guess he grunted.

"You smell like the woods and campfire smoke and sandalwood and some kind of perfume. I love those smells! And you and I both smoke menthol cigarettes," Ed said.

"I wish you wouldn't smoke, Ed," Mr. Lilley said.

Uh, oh. I was certain that Mr. Lilley didn't approve of anyone's smoking. Damn! But I did notice that Ed's nose was really big as was his dad's, so I figured that was why he could detect all those scents.

We'd been in the car about 20 minutes when Ed said, "We're almost there. The name of the place is the Alibi."

I giggled at the name, and I'm almost certain that Mr. Lilley grunted again. And then I worried if I was going to be able to gracefully slide out of the car. The "what ifs" started up again. I wanted a cigarette.

We pulled into the parking lot of the Alibi, and there were only three cars in the lot. Hmmm? Not a very popular place on a Tuesday night, I guess.

"Thanks for the ride," I said, turning to Mr. Lilley.

He smiled, grunted, and said, "Have a good time. Call me when you're ready for me to come for you."

I was already dreading that ride. Ed gave me his hand to help me out. A gentleman. I made it out with my skirt covering my upper thighs, thank God.

The Alibi was what I would call a run-down neighborhood bar/lounge, except there was no neighborhood. Ed opened the door for me to go in first. The door creaked, needing oil in the hinges. The smell of stale beer hit me, and I remembered that bridge party in Lincoln, Nebraska.

Two guys were sitting at the bar, and a woman bartender was chatting with them. She yelled at us to come in and sit anywhere.

"Place your drink order at the bar, and I'll bring them to your table," she called.

I was 18 1/2. I looked about 25, but I wasn't a drinker so no big deal. Ed asked what I wanted, and I told him 7UP or ginger ale. Already of age, Ed ordered himself a screwdriver.

Next to the bar was a room with tables and a dance floor with a large jukebox in the corner. No one else was in there—a dance floor to ourselves! I wasn't sure whether that was good or bad.

Nothing was playing on the jukebox, so after we picked out our table, we selected some songs. To this day, I still remember several of the songs we played. I'd just learned how to do the twist the year before, so my first selection was Chubby Checker's version. Ed chose "Pony Time" because he knew how to do the pony! It was fun picking out songs that we could sing along with like "Duke of Earl," "Where Have All the Flowers Gone," and "If I Had a Hammer."

Ed was funny, charming, and entertaining all at the same time. I was starting to relax. He was one of the funniest people I had ever met. He had great stories to tell, and he did hilarious comedic bits. We twisted. We ponied. We laughed and did the "Alley Cat" line dance. We sang "Shout" and did the arm-raising thing and crouched low when we had to get quieter. We looked at each other the whole time we danced! We laughed some more.

Then Ed went to the bar and ordered two more drinks. He made a side trip back to the jukebox and selected more songs. The next one up was Johnny Mathis's "Chances Are." He walked up to me, took a low bow, and said in a British accent, "M'lady, may I have this dance?" I thought he was definitely my white knight who had just ridden in on his white horse. I was being wooed. This all felt so good and so right.

"I could get used to this," I thought.

We started dancing slowly and a bit apart from each other. I thought maybe he was a little nervous because his hand seemed to be quite sweaty. He moved his wet hand to my waist, and I moved my right hand to his shoulder. He drew me in. I could feel his heart beating. Or maybe it was mine. We were no longer looking at each other because my cheek was resting on his shoulder, our bodies molded to each other's.

When "Chances Are" ended, we started to step away from each other but realized we couldn't. We were somehow stuck together at the waist. Our buckles had intertwined and would not come apart. We had to sidle, belly-to-belly, back to the table just as another couple entered OUR room. We smiled, laughed, and waved at them. They looked away, probably thinking we were nuts. We fiddled with the belts until finally they came apart. We danced and talked and laughed the night away.

Just before Ed called his dad to come and get us, he looked at me very seriously and said, "You do know that was a sign, don't you?"

"A sign?" I asked.

He looked me deeply in the eyes and said, "The belts. We were meant to be together."

The ride back to camp mirrored our ride to the bar. I was squished between those two men again, and the car reeked of chewing tobacco. Mr. Lilley asked if we had a good time, and we laughed and said that we had. Ed took my hand on the ride back. Mr. Lilley asked me a few questions about my life and family. Ed had filled me in on his dad's long teaching career, so I asked him several questions about his teaching. Conversation flowed among us, and I forgot about the chewing tobacco smell.

I wondered if Ed would kiss me goodnight. We got out of the car, and my skirt pulled up thigh high. I was mortified. What would his dad think? No doubt he'd think I was a slut. Before getting out of the car, I pulled my skirt down really fast,

"It was really pleasant getting to know you better, Mr. Lilley," I said. "Goodbye."

I was hoping Ed would find a way to sneak in a goodbye kiss without his dad noticing. He didn't kiss me goodnight, but he took my hands in his and said, "I can't wait to see you again, Mary. I'm anxious to get to know you better. Thanks for the wonderful evening."

"Me, too!" I said.

I was being wooed, and it felt good.

We were married two years later. Ed was my first true love, and I loved him until the day he died.

Ed and I wanted a small wedding of maybe 50 people. Mom had a different script, and she won. I had learned to pick my battles! Her invitation list had 275 people on it. We didn't want alcohol served at the reception at our house. Mom had a different script. She wanted to serve her famous champagne punch. She won. See a pattern here? One of the reasons I wanted to marry was to escape the control of my mother. I got hives when I talked about her. She adored Ed. However, he knew her true colors and was not intimidated by her.

A few words about virginity until your wedding night: It's way overrated. Thanks a lot, Mom, for that script. I think I was 14 years old when she first told me that *Saving yourself until your wedding night is the most loving gift you can give your husband. I was glad that I did.* I interpreted this to mean that any business between a guy and a gal below the neck was taboo. Just to be clear, I had discovered my body when I was 12, but of course, I thought that I was the only one in the world who had done that. It was my secret. I lied about that to Ed. I denied ever touching myself, I felt so ashamed about it. And I wanted him to think that I was pure in every sense of the word. I was in my 30s before I could even utter the word "masturbation." A few words about masturbation: It's way underrated.

So, because I was a virgin, Mom thought it would be a

good idea for me to see her gynecologist for a pelvic exam before my wedding to be sure that Ed would fit in there. I'd never seen an adult penis, so what did I know? I was mortified. But I went because I was terrified that I would bleed to death on my wedding night if I didn't.

Your first pelvic exam is pretty traumatic.

"Mary, relax. Relax," the doctor kept saying.

My knees wouldn't spread. I'd held them together for a really long time—years, in fact. Dr. Argus confirmed that I was too small and that the hymen was intact. Well, I knew that.

He said that he was going to have to cut the hymen and give me instructions on how to stretch myself with my fingers. He proceeded to deflower me with a small scalpel, which I felt. I neglected to tell him that I have a really slow clotting time, and he ended up having to apply pressure to the cut for 10 minutes. He tried making small talk with his hand between my legs. Really?!

"Please don't talk," I said and started to cry.

The doctor tried comforting me by apologizing.

"I mean it. Please don't talk," I repeated.

I thought I was going to bleed to death right there on the table. I'd die a virgin. Well, except I didn't feel like a virgin anymore. The doctor shut up.

He sent me home with finger-stretching ointment and wished me well with my marriage. I hemorrhaged 24 hours later. Mom panicked, and Dad drove me back to Dr. Argus, who then stitched up my hymen. He told me to keep stretching. I updated Ed on all of these goings-on, and he obviously had some concerns about our wedding night. I guessed he might have a big penis based on his nose size, but

I didn't ask him, because I didn't want him to know I knew the word "penis."

On June 14, 1964, Ed and I had a beautiful wedding in the garden at Beulah Presbyterian Church in Churchill, Pennsylvania, a suburb of Pittsburgh. The music, which Mom picked, of course, was lovely. I included eight of my best friends to be an "ivy rope chain" with English ivy that Mom and I picked from her garden. Each woman carried a daisy nosegay along with the ivy chain. My sister, Marcia, was my matron of honor.

Our dresses were made of cotton chambray, designed to our specifications. Marcia's was a soft teal, and mine was pure white, of course. I'd been told that only virgins were allowed to wear white. Guess who told me that?

We spent a two-night honeymoon at Jennerstown Playhouse and Inn, where Ed had done summer stock theater for a few summers.

As part of my trousseau, I had a beautiful white peignoir set, perfect for a wedding night. I didn't want to take it off, since no one had ever seen me naked except my parents and sister. I finally removed the robe, with the nightgown so sheer you could see my nipples. Ed hugged me and said soothing words, knowing that I was a stressed-out mess because of my hymen debacle. We forwent our marriage consummation until the following night, during which I worked at relaxing so much that I peed the bed. There is nothing less romantic and more embarrassing than to pee the bed the first time you make love. We tried to go to sleep, but we got the giggles and laughed all night long. Even more embarrassing was realizing that the maid service would know someone peed the bed!

Ed and I were both off from work for the summer. As a

teacher, Ed was clearing $150 every two weeks. I'd completed my job at the Pittsburgh YWCA teaching swimming. We needed money, so we applied for summer jobs. We had hoped to have found life-guarding jobs at a gorgeous resort where we could also honeymoon for the summer. I'd completed my water safety instructors certification at the University of Nebraska, and Ed had his senior life saving certificate, so we were a perfect couple for those jobs. No such luck.

We heard word of mouth from a Camp Riamo friend that the directors were looking for two waterfront staff. We decided that was going to be our honeymoon destination.

For the rest of the summer at the camp, our living accommodations weren't so perfect. For nine weeks, we lived in one of those three-sided shacks and slept on two rusted metal cots pushed together. They made lots of squeaky noises if you rolled over–let alone had sex. On the cots were straw tick mattresses. A canvas tarp had been hung for us on the open side of the shack for privacy, I suppose. It blew in the wind. We shared the outhouse with the directors.

Our memorable honeymoon summer was made up of more laughter, lots of folk singing, and enjoying the Girl Scouts and other staff members. But things didn't seem to be as I'd expected as far as love-making. It was pleasant, and we both satisfied each other in a non-exciting way. Same foreplay. Same position. Same falling asleep afterward. What bothered me was that Ed didn't want me to initiate sex, and as a result, we made love once a week or less. He also didn't want to talk about it. This was not the script that I was familiar with. That script had been based on some things I heard from friends or read. I wanted sex a couple of times a day.

Another factor impacting our love-making was Ed loved being with the other staff in the evenings around the campfire, telling his stories and relishing the admiration, attention, and idolization everyone had for him. He was funny, entertaining, persuasive, and charismatic—a poet and a dreamer. He was a combination of Leo Buscaglia, Kahlil Gibran, and Frederico Fellini, and he had the voice of God. He mesmerized anyone who would listen to him, including me. But most of all, Jim Gamble.

Jim was a student of Ed's and an actor prodigy. The camp director had been looking for a handyman, and Ed suggested Jim, who needed the work. He was hired immediately after his interview. Ed liked being Jim's mentor, and they enjoyed time together in the afternoons during our rest time before dinner. This time didn't include me.

At first that was okay because I needed some time to myself. But by the end of the summer, I was a bit jealous of Jim for the time that Ed wanted to spend with him. I didn't know how to talk with Ed about it. I started to have feelings of insecurity and fear that I loved Ed more than he loved me. Then I felt hurt.

I got so angry that we hardly touched each other the three weeks before we left to come home. I then felt really unhappy. How could this be? We'd only been married for two months. Our honeymoon was over. Ed went back to work, and I went back to college at Duquesne University for a bachelor of science degree in music education with a major in voice and a minor in piano.

Things became more strained between us, and we communicated less and less. I was certain that marriage counseling could help us and that Ed could really use it. He knew I was unhappy, but he did nothing to show me he loved me.

"If only you would make love to me more often, I'd be happy," I used to say.

Ed would go silent when I talked like that. Occasionally, he would say, "I don't want to feel controlled by what you want."

I never quite got that. He agreed to go to counseling, and we found a great counselor, Mildred Shagum. After the first two sessions, she suggested we have separate sessions for a while. I fully expected her to say, "Ed, when would be a good time to see you next week," but instead she said, "Mary, I'd like to schedule you for a few times over the next several weeks."

I would have said, "What the fuck?" but I didn't talk like that then. I was a people-pleaser, so I said, "Sure."

My throat started to tighten up, and my eyes began to burn. I wouldn't even look at Ed. I thought he might look smug. We were silent the whole way home in our yellow sun-roofed VW Beetle, which smelled of fermented rice that had been thrown at us when we got in the car to leave for our honeymoon. It reminded me of the fermented smells at Camp Riamo, and I remembered the laughter. I missed the laughter.

At my first counseling session, Mildred wanted to talk about my mother. I wanted to talk about Ed. She knew I was unhappy and that I felt Ed didn't love me. I whined to her about why I was upset that she didn't schedule Ed to come see her when it was Ed that needed the help. In the end, Ed went to one more session by himself, and I saw Mildred for two years.

I learned that I'd been pretty screwed up heading into my marriage. I was blinded by love and a fairytale with a "happily ever after" ending. At the same time, I was escaping living with my parents by marrying Ed. I learned that Ed was showing me he loved me in a myriad of ways. Even though he seldom said I love you, I knew he did. I needed to detach from my mother and erase the tapes that belonged to her.

Within the next few years, I graduated from Duquesne University and got a job teaching elementary music in Penn Hills, a Pittsburgh suburban school. I loved my job and was good at it. I made lifelong friends from that era.

Ed was involved in directing the junior and senior class plays and musicals at Springdale High School. He was brilliant at directing. Mother, who had theater experience as both an actress and a director, was in awe of his work with those high school kids. His undertakings included *The Crucible, Tea and Sympathy, Mr. Roberts, Teahouse of the August Moon,* and *The Miracle Worker.* His students adored him, and they would hang out with us at our apartment on the weekends.

We spent four summers working at Camp Lend-a-Hand, a residential Easter Seal Society camp near Conneaut Lake, Pennsylvania. Ed and I started out as boys and girls directors, and then he became the camp director, and I headed up the waterfront job. We grew further apart that last summer, and I'd never felt so lonely.

We'd been talking about starting a family, but Ed resisted having sex by the calendar. He felt he couldn't be spontaneous that way. But we tried to get pregnant once a month for six months, regardless of how Ed felt, because he really wanted a family, too.

One fine day, a Mother Earth-type mother of one of my piano students made me an omelet with fresh pumpkin blossoms from her garden. She promised that this would help me conceive. After six months of trying, we conceived two days after I ate that omelet. Ed and I questioned the science behind that old wives' tale. That was the last time Ed and I made love.

I loved being pregnant. I felt fabulous and beautiful. I was healthy and worked out. Ed and I were both excited about becoming parents. He was going to be my childbirth coach, which was rather rare in 1971, so we took classes on how to have a baby.

The classes are quite different from the real thing. My water broke four weeks before my due date, and I hadn't learned how to push yet. We missed the last two classes! My body didn't want to go into labor, so I was induced.

Labor hurt like hell. No one told me that when you're induced, your contractions are just as painful in the beginning as they are in the end. I never screamed or told Ed he was a son-of-a-bitch. He was a fabulous coach. Sixteen hours later, Jessica Kate Lilley was born—6 pounds, 13 ounces, and 20 inches long. She was yellow from jaundice, and we thought she looked tan and healthy! They treated her with a bilirubin lamp, and I had a couple of lessons in breastfeeding. They sent us home. OMG. I knew nothing about being a mother.

Jessica was only 18 months old when Ed asked me to sit down because he needed to have a difficult conversation with me. He took a deep breath.

"I love you. Just know that," he said.

I took a deep breath. Then he said that he didn't know whether he was bisexual or homosexual.

I was stunned. I'm sure you are not. How had I not seen this coming? I'm sure that my counselor, Mildred Shagam, probably knew.

Well, I knew that Ed was very close to Jeff, a good friend who taught at the same alternative high school as he did. Ed shared with me that he'd been having an affair with him for a couple of months. Ed admitted that he initiated that.

In retrospect, there were lots of signals, but I was quite blind and naïve. In everything else, Ed was so honest with me. I believe though that on the topic of his sexuality, he'd been as honest with me as he was with himself. He told me he'd been struggling for several years about who he was on several different levels. He was so excited to have discovered his sexuality. He wanted me to be happy for him.

What the fuck? I didn't say that out loud yet. But I thought about it very loudly.

Ed wanted to stay married. Really?! I was nonplussed. He said that he was happy with me. He wanted the best of two worlds.

"How utterly selfish," I thought.

I was torn apart.

Ed had read Fritz Perls's *Gestalt Therapy Verbatim*, and I happened to be in a Gestalt support group, run by Dr. Miller. I suggested to Ed that we schedule an appointment with Dr. Miller to discuss, thinking that having a third person in a relationship wasn't a very good idea.

I immediately started fearing that I wasn't enough of a woman for Ed. I wasn't sexy enough. I was 30 pounds overweight. I was hurt. Sad. Mad. I felt that he had stayed with me to show the world he was "normal." I felt used. I shared all of my feelings with Ed.

"I can understand why you feel that way,." he kept saying.

This was a teeny tiny bit reassuring to me.

Our appointment was scheduled for October 31, 1972. Halloween night. It was snowing lightly. We didn't talk the whole way there. Ed knew I was hurt, sad, and mad.

After Dr. Miller heard our story, he said, "If you want this marriage to work, and it sounds as if you both do, you'll not be able to continue your relationship with Jeff for a predetermined time, Ed, while you work on these issues. There cannot be a third person in the picture if you want your marriage to work. Do you both understand this?"

We both said yes.

That was about it. I was so glad that Ed agreed. He wasn't as selfish as I'd thought. I was more than willing to do the hard work to save our marriage.

When we got home, I asked Ed how long we should give ourselves to work on this.

"I'm not willing to give up seeing Jeff," he said.

"What the fuck?" I said, this time out loud!

I was shocked and stunned. We were standing facing each other at the time. He reached out to comfort me saying he was sorry. I threw his arms away from me.

"Don't you dare try to comfort me! You have no right! I'm done. Through. I can't live like this. I've been way too lonely for too long," I said, through tears, hurt, and rage.

We actually went to bed together. We didn't say a word. I couldn't stop crying, but more surprisingly, I couldn't stop shaking or catch my breath. I later learned that was my first panic attack! I finally got up.

"I can't stay here tonight. I'm going to my parents' house," I said.

I grabbed some overnight things, called them, and left. That was the second time in our marriage that I'd left him one night to be away from the pain of loneliness. The first time was when we were at Camp Lend-A-Hand, having only been married two years.

This time, we'd been married for 8 1/2 years.

My family surrounded me and actually gave me the comfort I needed. I was hugged and kind of rocked back and forth by my mother, and Dad patted me on my back.

My youngest brother, Steve, who was 17 at the time, was so sweet. He wasn't too sure how to react to my story, but he knew I needed comforting. He may have hugged me the tightest.

In a crisis when my mother didn't quite know what to do, she felt it necessary to call the church minister. They arranged for a meeting at my parents' house the following day. I didn't know this minister, but Mom spoke highly of him and said that he was wise. At this point in my life, I was pretty much an agnostic, so I wasn't really sure how this time was going to go.

When the minister arrived, he suggested that we have a private session, so we went downstairs to the studio where he sat on a chair and I sat on the daybed. I told him the story and waited for him to say some consoling words.

Instead, he said, "I can understand that you might feel some shame when a marriage fails and ..." He talked on, but I was stuck on his assumption that I felt shame. Well, what the fuck? I felt no shame. I felt every emotion BUT shame.

He asked if I would like to pray with him.

"No thanks," I said.

Later, I told my parents what he said, and they were a bit surprised, too. Needless to say, I felt even more rage than I had before.

Our friends were shocked that our marriage had failed. We were considered the ideal couple! Only my closest friends knew about my loneliness. They weren't surprised.

I'd taken the year off to have Jessica. I had no job except for a handful of piano students, and I knew that I would get custody of her. I'd be generous with visitation—every other weekend and one night a week. I would need child support. And I would file for divorce on the grounds that my husband was gay.

I learned soon enough that it would go on public record and that Ed would never be able to serve in the armed forces if I did—and that the world would know. I couldn't do that to him.

Four months later, I filed for a Pennsylvania no-fault divorce. My dad was my corroborating witness. I remember that we went out to lunch afterward, and he suggested that Jessica and I move in with them. I thanked him and said, "Absolutely not!"

Later, Mother agreed that it would not be a good idea. Two women under one roof does not make for a happy home. At least it wouldn't have been one in our case.

Our marriage was over. Ed and Jeff got an apartment together in Shadyside, an artsy area of Pittsburgh, and I found an apartment in Oakmont, a suburb about 20 minutes away. Ed's dad felt bad for me and came and helped me paint. Ed and Jeff helped with my move. We were civil.

I took on 35 piano and three voice students, and I was still barely holding it together financially. Ed's child support was only $150 a month, which we needed, but he was lousy at paying it either at all or on time. We had no medical insurance.

But in Jessica's eyes, Ed was a great dad. He became the parent who did all the fun, creative stuff with her. He built her a puppet theater and made all her Halloween costumes. I had given him my sewing machine, and he became a master costume maker for her. He took her to Disney World when she was four years old.

On the other hand, I did the mundane, day-to-day stuff, for example: got Jessica ready for daycare, did the grocery shopping, went to the playground, put Jessica to bed, and read her a story and sang several lullabies. I couldn't afford lavish trips to Florida, so I took her to the shore or camping. And I was the one who held her and sang her to sleep while she cried missing her dad.

Twenty-eight years after Ed and I divorced, I received this six-page, hand-written letter from him. Because he repeated himself a lot, I condensed it.

August 5, 2000

Mary,

Shortly after Kate was born, Jess gave me a book called *Grandfather Remembers*. It is organized to include a history of my childhood, my young adult life, and my life all the way up until now. It includes a section on Values I Hold Dear. It immediately confronted me with the job (and privilege) of deciding what I would choose to share of my values. Thoughts started to flow about what I would want her to know about me, my character, my past ... and which parts I would wish I could hide – parts of my life of which I am deeply ashamed. Then it came to me that standing above them all because it changed other people's lives so negatively was my having broken the vows of our marriage. I broke a sacred vow. At that point in my life, I had never sworn to anything before.

I was extremely shallow and very self absorbed, AND I was powerfully affected by you. I was very attracted to you–your looks, your humor, your love of life–your spirit. I loved you more than I had ever loved anyone else before. Even though I HAD seen the signs inside myself of something that was loathsome and compelling that I knew I needed to keep in the dark, I counted on being able to suppress and hopefully leave behind this stronghold in the sacred act of marriage. But I had not brought my life under the authority of God first ... so the vows were doomed. I made vows I did not keep. I swore to love, cherish, protect, and accompany you 'til death. You, Mary, and you, Jessica ... a covenant with God witnessed by my family, your family, and a community of friends. I did so with all the honesty I could muster in a heart still hiding from God. You, Mary, took those vows, and I experienced you as ready to partner me, your love of me, you gave me your devotion, you intended to walk with me the rest of our days. You were a wonderful wife! You were absolutely the wife God intended for me—gave to me. I loved you. You were a wonderful partner. I cherish the memories of our early family life. I grew very ashamed about my neglect more and more of your emotional and physical needs. I neglected my spiritual needs.

More and more of me went underground. In the name of "finding myself" or "being who I really was," I went off to follow a path of addiction, living in the shadows, adoring false gods, and desperately seeking the Divine in all the wrong places.

Leaving you and Jess was the most hurtful, sad, and sinful act I have ever committed. I had no business leaving the partnership we had formed and responsibilities of raising a child. I broke a sacred vow. I broke up a family. The aftermath of that is impossible to measure on my own, yours, and Jessica's lives. What an irresponsible, unthinkable, selfish thing for me to have done. I left you with a child, no real job, and very meager and intermittent support. I don't know how you handled it emotionally or physically. You took care of Jess, created a new career, and continued to be civil to me. You are an *amazing* woman!

I walked away from not only my responsibilities but from the gift God had given me—a life with you and Jessica as a family. I ask your forgiveness for all of the broken pieces I left you to pick up and to do it as a single mother. I take responsibility for the pain, the stress, and the wounding. I ask forgiveness for any burden this may have caused in your relationship with Jess or in Jess's with you.

We are a broken family. I thank you for all you did all those years to provide for Jess, both all you could muster as the mother and also all you could fill in for a father who was off somewhere neglecting his family. I appreciate all you did to allow her to love me and for not pouring bitterness on that love. That required unbelievable grace. Because you were the primary parent, you had to sit with all the complaints and sinews. Jess idealized me (the absent one). You still have not reaped the harvest for all that you labored to plant alone and exhausted. You shall. You shall!

We are led by a child...

The birth of Kate and witnessing Jess as a wife and as a mother has started all kinds of self-examination and awareness of my relationship to God. The book, a gift from our daughter, sent me running toward repentance and into the arms of God. I couldn't imagine He could forgive me and love me even after all. I have been forgiven. I am reborn. I am saved, but I will still witness the aftermath in the real world of my sins (in people's lives). I am facing up to the pain I created.

This is why I'm asking you to forgive me. I've started with you because you loved me and accepted my promise and turned your life toward our future. This is the future my behavior brought us.

I want you to know that I pray for you and Bill

when I pray for my family because in its broken forms you're, of course a part of my family, and I have been greatly blessed by your presence in my life.

I pray for your relationship with Jess to grow and flow and bloom. You are both such precious souls, and both were intended to have a glorious celebrative life with each other. I pray for a healing of any pain my sins may have created in your relationship. God gave you each the joy of loving and being loved by the other, honoring and being honored and the assurance that you both are loved *perfectly* by God.

Mary, when I married you, I had not given authority to God to be in charge of my life. I was convinced I could do it my way. That was very stupid and very wrong. I have acknowledged God's authority and have a new life. I thank God for you, Mary, for who you were to me then and for who you are to me now.

I hope you can forgive me.

I love you,

Ed

I forgave Ed. It was easy after all those years and because of the honesty and humility in this letter. We became friends. My last time with Ed was spent singing camp songs. It was a loving time together, even as he was dying of Alzheimer's disease. I never stopped loving him.

8

PROJECT DISCOVERY

In the fall of 1973, I joined Parents Without Partners along with a good neighbor friend of mine who had been single-parenting for 17 years. Anna Mae was my single-parenting mentor. Going out was new to her. Well, it was new to me, too, but I was adventuresome and looking forward to being social. And I eventually wanted to get laid. That was the beginning of my journey to uncover my own sexuality, which I shall call Project Discovery!

I was pretty stupid and naïve about sex and dating as a single parent. I had not read any romance novels. The raciest thing I read in high school was Jane Austen's *Pride and Prejudice*. I looked for our copy of the *Kama Sutra* but couldn't find it. Ed must have gotten custody of that. Over the next three years, I discovered some important things:

1. Many men who only wanted a romp in the hay or had been around the block, so to speak, didn't want to have anything to do with me until I had

a couple of years of experience under my belt, so to speak.

2. Some men knew very little about pleasing a woman. Thank you, Ed, for all the times you pleased me.

3. Many men thought that if they took you to dinner or for drinks and dancing, you owed them.

4. Many men didn't know how to kiss. But, I took the time to teach them. I learned that some men can't learn how to kiss.

5. Some men know only one position for sex. Some know way too many.

6. Some men, I'm sure, were great at sex, but they were 30 years older than I and wanted to teach me. I had a little bit of trouble with that.

7. All I wanted in a man was someone who liked to screw and was handy with tools around the house. My standards were pretty low.

8. Some men lied to you and said they were single, but actually they were either married or were temporarily separated from their wives–like for the night.

9. When you have sex for the first time since your divorce, you feel a bit guilty like you're cheating on your ex-husband. That feeling only lasts about a half-hour, so to speak.

10. Size doesn't matter.

11. I learned that some men are very adept with their hands, and that's okay.

12. It takes a long time to feel comfortable naked with someone you don't know very well.

13. Long underwear on a man is not sexy.
14. Some men are givers, other men are takers, and some are both.
15. I became comfortable and adept at more than one position.
16. I learned that I was horny almost all the time! Heck, I was in my early thirties!
17. I learned how to please a man, so to speak.

I met Martin at Parents Without Partners, and we started dating exclusively. Martin was simple, as in uncomplicated. He was tall—6'6"—dark, and handsome. My mother said he looked like a matinee idol. That was the 1930s name for a soap opera star.

He was a widower with two children. His wife died of cirrhosis of the liver from alcohol, which left wounds on all three of them. I was a nurturer, and this fit with my dysfunction in thinking I could love their wounds away. And I finally got laid. He liked to screw, and he was fairly handy with tools. Martin fell in love with me, and I fell in love with his family. He had a son, David and a daughter, Judi. Judi was a delight and was four years older than Jessica, 2 1/2 at the time. We all really enjoyed the feeling of family.

I thank Martin for introducing me to a couple of my bucket list items. I thought it was about time I went to a porn movie just to see what it was like. I begged him to take me. We ended up double dating with my best friend, Kathy, and her husband, Bob. The theater was in the Strip district in Pittsburgh, famous for its adult entertainment venues. I wasn't ready for how large everything looked on the huge screen and those up close and very personal camera angles. Oh, my! Kathy and I ended up laughing out loud at most everything we saw. We also said OH. MY. GOD a lot! Our guys kept telling us to keep it down that there were other people–both of them were men by the way-in the theater with paper cups. A little too loudly I asked why they would have paper cups. I hadn't seen a snack bar when we came in. At that moment, one of the men in the audience shushed me and said, "Be quiet." This made Kathy and me giggle, which we tried to muffle, but the guys decided they would have to get us out of there. But I wanted to know how the movie ended. Martin said that there was no plot, so the ending wasn't going to mean anything.

"Well, everyone comes and goes home, and that's the end," Bob said.

We all laughed at that.

The other bucket list item was to have sex in a car. I thought that would be hot. Martin was game. He had a station wagon, and he put the backseat down earlier that day. We were at a Parents Without Partners weekend at a camp in the mountains. We put the kids to bed and waited for them to go to sleep. Then we sneaked out to the car. It was after midnight.

We crawled into the back of the station wagon, took off our bottoms, and could NOT find a position that could accommodate Martin's long legs. We got creative about how to do it and proceeded to struggle and laugh. We were both uncomfortable and not particularly enjoying the process. It certainly wasn't hot and steamy. The shocks were bad, and every movement we made made them screech and squeak.

After quite some time, we actually finished up, and the squeaking stopped. We were breathing pretty heavily when all of a sudden we heard applause from the porch of one of the cabins. We were mortified, but we laughed, pulled our pants back on and crawled out of there while they were still applauding. Being the dramatic type that I am, I took a deep curtsey and waved like a queen might. Martin was very shy, and he couldn't even make eye contact with them when we walked by.

The next night, Martin proposed. I said I wasn't sure—that I needed time. He gave me a ring.

"I'm sorry, but it's only a cubic zirconia. I'll get you a real diamond when you say 'yes,'" he said.

He wanted me to know that his proposal was a risky big step because his mother said that because I wasn't Catholic, she would kill herself if we got married. Well, that was a fine how'dya do! It didn't take too long after that to realize that Martin wasn't the forever man for me. It would only be a matter of time that I would break his and our children's hearts. The thought of that tore me apart.

Then I was hired by Westinghouse Electric Corporation into their graduate student course. In those years, large corporations that had government contracts needed to comply with Affirmative Action. Our class was a diverse mixture of different degrees and colors and two genders. My dad was proud yet wondering how I would do in the electrical field because my degree and teaching experience were all in the music field. I was not sure how I would do either. But, I knew one thing: There were a lot of men, and I was going to enjoy working with men for a change. So many men, so little time.

One night, in my living room, three months into my graduate student course assignment, I told Martin that I thought our relationship wasn't going to work. I decided that I was going to work toward a career path in Westinghouse's Industry Products Company and that I wouldn't have time for a relationship.

He wasn't heart broken. He was enraged, pushed me to the floor, grabbed my hair, and pounded my head on the floor. I couldn't believe what was happening.

"Have you ever been raped? How would you like to be raped?" Martin shouted.

Panic set in, but I was able to fight him off. Thank goodness he was drunk.

"NO!!!! GET OFF OF ME! DON'T TOUCH ME!" I yelled. Rough water!

It was as if Martin was slapped back into reality. He got off of me, stood up, and left immediately. I shook for hours, fearful of what could have happened but knowing the breakup was the right thing to do.

Martin has since passed away as did his son, but his daughter, Judi, found me on Facebook. She seems happy. I'm so relieved.

9

I MARRIED A FORTUNE 100 COMPANY

Westinghouse was my next serious love. It was the mid-1970s, and I'd been working for Westinghouse's Industry Products Company in sales and marketing. I'd been promoted to assistant sales engineer and moved from Pittsburgh to Allentown, Pennsylvania. Yes, of Billy Joel fame!

Project Discovery bumped up a notch on many different levels, not just sexual. I was part of a man's world. I loved working with the guys and becoming one of them. I was often told that I had balls. I took this as a compliment. I developed a sailor's mouth. I loved the success I felt in my career: I was promoted five times in 14 years and broke some glass ceilings for other women. I loved the travel, where I had a guy in every port—non-business related—State College, Williamsport, Bloomsburg, Danville, and Scranton. I loved the customers, the distributors, and electrical contractors. Well, the ones who gave me business! I even loved the equipment that I sold: panelboards, switchgear, motor control centers, transformers, and other electrical distribution equipment. Life was an exciting adventure. I thrived on the bidding deadlines. I was good at the negotiations.

And I liked flirting, which was harmless with the guys I worked with—or at least I thought so at the time. There was one other female in the office—a 60-ish administrative assistant. In retrospect, I'm sure that I offended her. And I believe that she was a bit jealous of my youth and the fun relationship I had with the guys. Or at least I thought so at the time.

Our sales office was laid out with the desks all facing one direction, toward the manager's office. There were two desks, side by side, on the window side of the office and one desk on the wall side with an aisle in between, which led to the back of the office where the customer service guys and the restrooms were. My desk was one of the front desks, which meant that every time I had to see one of the customer service people or use the restroom, everyone would know and have a comment.

"Oh, look, Mary's gonna take another leak."

"Mary's heading to the head again."

"Wonder what all she does in there?"

"Gettin' any?"

"There she goes again. She's PMS-ing."

"Hey, Mary, you're kinda bitchy today!"

This went on daily, ad infinitum. I always had a quick comeback line.

Them: "Gettin' any?"

Me: "Three times last night."

Them: "Wonder what she does in there?"

Me: I read … (pause) … interesting things."

These comments would occur both on my way to the back of the office and returning to my desk. It was a game that we played. Today, it would be called harassment—on both sides.

One day, I made a trip to the restroom, accompanied by the comments and my retorts. When I came back out and walked down the aisle, one of the guys whooped and hollered, "Hey, Mary! You've got a tail!"

I ignored him.

"What's that you're dragging behind you?" asked another coworker, laughing,

I turned around and much to my horror, I was trailing a stream of toilet paper! I blushed as I turned to rush back to the restroom.

"I meant to do that! I wanted to be sure you guys weren't sleeping on the job!" I said.

"Right. Sure," they answered.

They never let me forget that, and for a couple of months they would say, "Oh, look, Mary's trailing toilet paper again," even when I wasn't.

Being around men all day made me horny. I would make a daily trip to the restroom to deal with that, so to speak. I imagine that some of the guys did the same. I became much less naive about things and learned that many married men hit on women. I saw it happen at district and regional meetings and conventions. I was a bit disillusioned about that. I didn't like to think that so many married men cheated on their wives. I never would have wanted that to happen to me again.

I changed my behavior slightly. I stopped saying, "Nice ass," when one of the guys would walk past my desk. I was beginning to evolve, becoming more professional with my coworkers. It was a slow process. Two years later, I was promoted to the outside sales engineer position. This was a huge deal for a woman in the electrical construction industry.

Every Friday, the guys and I would go out after work for happy hour and to compare notes on how our week went. Three drinks later, we would all say stuff that we sometimes regretted the next day. For example, I told them that I had a guy in every port, and I didn't get paid to spend time with them. I'm sure they thought I was promiscuous. But I didn't know the meaning of that word until later.

My favorite booze was vodka—still is. I invented a drink that was two shots of vodka with half a lime squeezed in it- up. I was known for that drink, and they named it a "Mary Lilley." Alcohol was part of every business lunch, meeting, and of course, happy hour. And we almost all smoked.

I'll never forget a lunch I had with a contractor that lasted five hours. He drank about eight Manhattans, and I had four Mary Lilleys. Among many other subjects relating to the industry and equipment, we discussed a bill of mate- rial that I'd given him in hopes that I'd get some business from this well-known and successful contractor. I knew my price was right even though he wanted to negotiate a lower price. I stood firm. He got drunk, and I suggested that we go back to the office so I could get my car and go home. I prayed that he'd get us back to the office safely. He grabbed my thigh on the way back.

"If you sleep with me, I'll give you this order," he said.

I was horrified. I was also a bit scared because when we got to the office I had to go in to get my coat and briefcase. We went in. He didn't turn the lights on and started chasing me around the tables and desks. I couldn't see where my coat and briefcase were. I told him that I couldn't be bought and that I refused to even take the order.

"You'll be losing out on millions of dollars of future business if you don't fuck me," he said, his parting shot.

"I'll pass. Now turn on the damn lights and stay away from me!" I said.

He did as he was staggering around knocking over chairs in an effort to get to me. I moved too fast for him and left, furious. I'd never had to deal with that kind of behavior or "negotiation" before or after that in my career, and it made me sick.

During those early years with Westinghouse, I dated several Lehigh Valley men, one being David, the guy that Jessica hated. I met him at a singles dance, and we talked for three hours that night. My first date with him was memorable. He invited me to his house to roast hot dogs and marshmallows for S'mores in his fireplace. I like hot dogs, so that was one of the reasons why I said yes. David knew from our discussion that yellow was my favorite color. When I arrived at his house, I walked into a living room completely filled with a gross of inflated yellow balloons. That's 144 balloons. I was so excited to have found a man who could get creative about a date! I wondered if he liked to screw and was handy with tools. He did, and he was.

I was working for Westinghouse Electric Corporation, and David had been laid off from his job with Xarat as a project manager. David was bright. I introduced him to the branch manager of WESCO Reading - Westinghouse Electric Supply Company, the distributing arm of Westinghouse. The branch manager hired him as an inside sales person. I bring this up because this was one of two Westinghouse distributors in Reading. I called on both of them as customers. My dating David wasn't private information, and this was the first time I'd mixed business with pleasure. The other distributor found out and was angry about this relationship, which was totally understandable at the time, and eventually, David was transferred to WESCO Baltimore. I learned a lesson from this. It underscored why business and pleasure couldn't be mixed. I also learned that David was a user of people, and I grew tired of that. I should have listened to Jessica! Distance made it easy to end that relationship.

After that, I was much more careful in my flirting banter with my officemates—avoiding obvious sexual innuendo. Again, it was a slow evolution. I often had to laugh at their comments, but I started to limit my comeback lines. I read *Dress for Success* and started wearing more skirted suits and blouses.

I was still in love with Westinghouse, but it was a more

mature love. We'd shifted from the honeymoon to the committed trusting relationship. I was loyal to that company, and it merited my hard and successful work. It was an ideal give-and-take relationship, and I felt appreciated. I was offered an inside sales position at WESCO Camden, which would put me in a career path to becoming a branch manager. Months later, I was offered a created-just-for-me position as a Mid-Atlantic regional projects manager with an office in Bala Cynwyd, Pennsylvania. Months later, I was offered the branch manager position at WESCO Reading.

During the four Reading, Camden, and Bala Cynwyd years, I became more stressed with the pressure of these jobs. My blood pressure went up, and I was diagnosed with type 2 diabetes and osteoarthritis. I was actually promoted out of what I did best—my corporate sales engineer job. The Peter Principle, which states that **people are promoted to their level of incompetence**, had set in.

The WESCO Reading job chewed me up and spit me out. It was the first job that I ever had in which I didn't excel. I think my employees sensed I was unhappy. I cried my way to and from work. In 1990, I divorced Westinghouse and started my own business as a corporate image consultant. I never looked back.

At the same time, I also took a hiatus from dating so many men in so little time! Little did I know that the best was yet to come.

10

SOULMATE

It was the middle of September 1986, and a few of the leaves had started to change colors. The evenings had begun to cool off, and I was feeling fat and out of shape. I tipped the scales at 225 pounds—the size of a football player. From behind, with my short hair, broad shoulders, and narrow hips, I could *pass* for a football player. I decided to have a serious talk with myself about this state of affairs.

Healthy Mary: "Mary, what have you done to yourself? You're obese and out of shape. You've really let yourself go to pot. Do you want to live like this?"

Gone-to-pot Mary: "Of course, I don't want to live like this. I'm tired all the time, my clothes are getting tighter, and I hate my body."

Healthy Mary: "What do you want to do about it?"

Gone-to-pot Mary: "I suppose I should go on a diet and exercise. I've heard good things about the Atkins Diet. I hate exercise, like in the gym. I like to swim, but I don't want to have to pay the membership fee at the YWCA to use their pool. What can I do?"

Healthy Mary: "You used to love to square dance as a child! There's a singles square dance group that meets in Bethlehem. Why don't you do that?"

Gone-to-pot Mary: "I LOVE that idea! Thanks, Healthy Mary! That's what I'm going to do! I'm going to dance for exercise!

The Bachelors and Bachelorettes singles square dance group met at Eisenhower Elementary School in Bethlehem, Pennsylvania. This was a class specifically for beginners. I parked out front and questioned myself, "What was I thinking?" Oh, yes, to get exercise. I needed exercise. I was there, sitting in the car and kind of frozen, unable to get out of the car. I took a deep breath, opened the car door, and just sat there. Healthy Mary shouted at me, "GET THE HELL OUT OF THE CAR! YOU'RE GOING TO DO THIS!"

I made it out of the car and slowly walked to the entrance of the school. I felt a bit nervous about going in. I'm not sure why. Maybe because I didn't want to look stupid if I made mistakes dancing. I wasn't there to catch a man. At age 42, I was really happy with my carefree, single life. I'd experienced so many men in so little time that I'd worn myself out! I was taking a break and enjoying it.

I'd picked my outfit out based on comfort. I wore a tiered denim maxi skirt and a white, loose-fitting blouse, flats with leather soles, and minimal makeup. I entered the building and followed the sound of voices to the gymnasium. I entered the gym and immediately felt out of place.

Many of the women had on very unflattering, knee-length, full-ruffled skirts, which stood straight out from the waist because of the many crinolines underneath. I wouldn't be caught dead in one of those skirts. They looked like stupid tutus. Many of the blouses were scoop necked, almost off the shoulder. Others were plain colored or white short-sleeved shirts. They almost all wore scarves around their necks, some of which were bandana patterns. It was their uniform—or shall I call it a ridiculous costume?

Several friendly people greeted me and steered me to the membership person, sitting at a table. As we walked, I noticed the women outnumbered the men by about two to one. Almost all the men were dressed in jeans, Western shirts, and bolo ties, which was apparently *their* uniform.

Because I was in a gymnasium, all I could think about were the days that I was in elementary school where the gym teachers thought it would be a good idea to combine the boys' and girls' classes to teach us all how to do the box step. To me, this was a horrible idea. The teachers assigned the boys to the girls and to my horror, the boy who was chosen to be my partner, first of all, didn't want to be mine, and secondly, had really bad breath.

Just as I was giving the membership person my name and $5, a man went up to a microphone and announced it was time to get started. He introduced himself as Jake, the caller. He asked the beginners to raise their hands and then introduced the experienced square dancers, otherwise known as "angels." Angels were the guides to us beginners.

The caller asked us to get into a huge circle. The angels spaced themselves between the beginners. The hoedown-type music started, and he called to us to circle to the left eight steps, followed by circling to the right eight steps. And to repeat. The music stopped, and he taught the group how to do-se-do with the person on the right, then the left, an allemande left, and finally a grand right and left. He put the music back on, and he called a fun circle dance using all the things we'd learned. I was actually having fun!

About halfway through the dance, I noticed a man opposite me staring. As soon as I made eye contact with him, he would look away, as if he was embarrassed. This happened several times, and I was a little uncomfortable with it. We danced another circle dance and then broke up into eight-person squares. This man joined our square next to me as my corner. We practiced honoring our partners, crossing over, swinging our partners and corners, do-si-do-ing, and allemande left, grand right, and left. It was all coming back to me! My corner man had a very light touch but led well when I accidentally went the wrong way. He smiled. I did, too. I noticed that he wore jeans well.

At the end of the dance, the man introduced himself as Bill. He seemed a bit socially uncomfortable and shy. He was an angel and asked if I'd like to be his partner for the next set.

"Sure," I said.

Again, he gently led me through some steps that I hadn't remembered, and I felt grateful for his expertise in this Western style of square dancing, which was so different from the square dancing I did with my parents and in elementary school—the Hoedown style. This was much more structured and seemed a bit stiff to me, but hey, I was moving my ass and had some laughs when I screwed up!

Several weeks of dance classes passed, and Bill and I chatted a couple of times, mostly about square dancing, during the breaks. Then one night, he asked me out on a date. Because I wasn't in the market to be in a relationship, my first response was, "No, but thanks for asking."

A couple of more weeks passed, and Bill asked me out

again. I guess my thanks for asking me out before was an invitation to ask me again. I can't recall what I said, but I declined again. I saw him as a nice man who was polite and a square dance mentor, not dating material. I thought he was a bit square! And I really wasn't interested in dating anyone at that point in my life.

Well, this persistent man asked me out again, and again I said no. Would you believe he asked me out again? I was starting to admire his determination.

Here's what he said, "I'd like to know if you would come to Philadelphia with me to see a trombonist friend of mine play in a dance band. We could dance, and you'd have a chance to hear some great music."

Sheesh, no one had ever asked me out on a date like that. First of all, I was excited to know that he had a friend who played trombone and that she also happened to have a PhD in something like biophysics. Holy shit. I was intrigued. Impulsively, completely forgetting that I didn't want to date anyone, I said, "Sure, that sounds like fun!"

After I got home, I asked myself, "What the hell were you thinking?"

I thought I'd maybe made a mistake. I'd be spending several hours in the car with Bill, and I wasn't sure we'd have enough to talk about. Well, I didn't have to worry about that, we got lost looking for the lounge in northeast Philly. I was the navigator with the map with bad lighting. We finally arrived at the lounge in enough time to dance the last set. And by the way, we didn't dance very well together. I kept stepping on his toes, and he kept leading me forward, which put me off balance. Had a chance to meet Leslie, the very good trombonist who had a brilliant mind. She seemed to have a lot of admiration and respect for Bill. They had worked together at Penn. It was interesting to see him through someone else's eyes.

When we got back to Quakertown, where I'd left my car, as we were saying goodbye, Bill leaned in to kiss me. I was unprepared. It was quick, and I didn't respond very well. I was uncomfortable with this man I hardly knew. Though, I must say I was intrigued by him enough to maybe go out with him again. I'd seen a bit more of his kindness, gentleness, brilliance, and humor. I've always been drawn to bright men who are funny. I wanted to get to know Bill better as a friend.

The next week, Bill asked me to go to Godfrey Daniels, an intimate, folksingers' coffee shop-type place in Bethlehem. I'd heard of it and always had wanted to go, but never had.

Godfrey's has the feel of a speakeasy, and the seating is a combination of tables, chairs, and church pews. Bill chose a church pew. I realized later that it was because he wanted to sit next to me to put his arm around me, which he did about one-third of the way through the concert, which happened to be blues singer Rory Block. Surprisingly, I was comfortable with Bill's arm around my shoulder. But, then about halfway through the concert, Bill started a gentle massage on my shoulder. I'd been extremely stressed out about my job, and the tension was in my neck and shoulders.

At that moment I thought, "I could get used to this."

Afterward, we enjoyed talking about Rory's concert, and Bill bought me one of her CDs, which had my favorite song of hers on it, *Cool Drink of Water*. A nice gesture.

He drove me back home, and I surprised myself by inviting him in. More shoulder massage ensued along with neck massage and some kisses, lots of conversation about things like values, life's meaning for each of us …what's really important. He was just as curious about me as I was with him. I'd been with too many guys who never asked one question about me. Bill was like a breath of fresh air. I was starting to like being with Bill. It was easy to be with him. And no games. Whew! What a relief that was.

Bill and I were still square dancing every week–really enjoying it. I decided it was time to consider getting a tutu outfit! Bill and I went together, and I spent about $100 that day! The tutu crinolines were pretty expensive, and I needed two outfits. What had gotten into me, I haven't a clue.

A funny thing happened the first time I wore my Western clothes, as they were called, I danced better! I had fun grabbing the edge of my skirt and waving it back and forth when we sashayed around the square! I think that wearing that costume shifted me into a character who enjoyed square dancing more than I ever had. And it gave me permission to wear a tutu!

A major turning point in our relationship, which up until that point felt like a friendship with some necking, was when Bill invited me to come to his house for dinner to meet his family. Those attending were Bill's sister, Anne, who was temporarily living with him, his son, Warren, and Warren's wife, Lori.

I was a bit nervous when I arrived. I wasn't sure of his family's perception of our relationship. They all put me at ease. They'd been through this routine before with Bill's bringing girlfriends home to meet family. A few words about Bill's dating history: He dated a lot. At one point he was seeing a Jan, Jane, a Janet, and a Joan—all at the same time! Whew!

The dinner conversation flowed easily, and the food was good. Bill had done the shopping and cooking, and I was impressed. When it came time to clear the table, I asked Lori, "How about you and I do the cleanup?"

She agreed, but then I added this comment to Bill, "We will do this on one condition. That you entertain us while we do it."

Without hesitation, Bill said, "Alright. Will do." He immediately left the kitchen and returned five minutes later with a book in hand and gillies on his feet. Gillies are soft dance shoes that you wore for Scottish country dancing. He proceeded to do a soft shoe and read e. e. Cummings poetry to us as we loaded the dishwasher.

I thought to myself, "I REALLY like this man."

I decided right then and there that I wanted this man in my life. Period. I knew then that he was unique, special, funny, gentle, bright, thoughtful, and sweet. "Be open for whatever this relationship might be," I told myself.

And did I mention that he founded his own software consulting company? He let me know early on that he wasn't rich. Good thing that wasn't important to me. I was in a high-powered career when we met, making enough money to support myself and my daughter.

Four months after we met, Bill and I knew that we were meant to be together—forever. We planned on getting married. Bill and his former wife had been separated for seven years, and even though Bill filed for divorce, it got stuck in the process. When we made the decision to be together, Bill contacted his lawyer, and the wheels were in motion. The process of their divorce took about two years. Bill had moved in with me in August 1987. My dad was horrified and judgmental, but my mother was accepting. She loved Bill. We were married May 27, 1989.

Although looking back, I met Bill at the right time for me, but it was the most turbulent of Jessica's years. In the beginning, she and Bill didn't connect. I'm sure that she resented his presence in our house. They were cordial with each other. They peacefully coexisted.

As the years went by, I've watched Jessica warm to Bill. She has seen his love for me, and she gets it. She's happy for us. She gives Bill carefully chosen birthday and Father's Day cards to tell him how much she appreciates him. Once, when she was doing some online dating, she told me she'd met a really nice guy.

"I think I've met my Bill Thompson," she said.

I understood that she didn't mean he was exactly like Bill, but that he was a good, honest, kind, sweet, nerd who loved her. She saw Bill's love for me and wanted that for herself. This was a supreme compliment to Bill. Yes, Bill is a nerd, and I say that in the most affectionate way, but he is also a very loving and thoughtful man.

On the other hand, I'd started to develop a loving relationship with Bill's two sons, Warren and Steve. We don't see Warren very much because he lives in Tennessee.

But Steve and I are very close. We live 45 minutes away from Steve, his wife, Sharon, and Connor, our fifth grandchild. I feel that all my grandchildren and their spouses and significant others are like my own blood relatives: Kayleigh and Nick, Jeff and Rebecca, Eric and Dan, Kate and Mike. I love them with all my heart. And we can't forget our two great granddaughters, Jada, and Jeff and Rebecca's daughter, Delilah.

In our 25th year of marriage, I earned a new lease on life with my gastric by-pass surgery and resulting 120-pound weight loss. I was reborn physically, and I now loved my body in a whole new way, loose skin and very saggy boobs and wrinkled knees and all!

I recall one night while Bill and I were spooning. He reached over for my breast and kept feeling around.

"I can't find your boob. Where did it go?" he asked.

"It's lying on the bed beside me," I said.

Bill thought that was hilarious.

A few words about Bill: He was the perfect husband and support system for me throughout my entire yoyo dieting years and weight loss journey, although he had quite a bit of trepidation about my having such a serious surgery. Today, we've been together for 35 years. Since my doctor warned me about the possibility of an early death in 15 years, I've lived 23 more years. Yay!

Bill never mentioned my size or what or how much I was eating. And he was always attracted to me. After the doc told me I had 15 years to live was the first time that Bill ever said to me that he'd been concerned about my health. He loved me through thick and thin. Bill is quite a guy. A keeper.

Bill and I are two imperfect people in an almost perfect marriage. One of Bill's minor faults is that he's not a great handyman, but he is a great lover, in the broadest sense of the word—thoughtful, giving, caring, sexy. He helps me stay grounded and brings calm to my sometimes frantic episodes. He is my soulmate, and I will love him until the day I die. Bill, thank you for loving me more perfectly than I've ever been loved.

PART III

LEAVING TRAILS OF LIGHT

"Go out into the world today and love the people you meet. Let your presence light new light in the hearts of others."
—Mother Teresa

11

MARY SUNSHINE TO MARY STARSHINE

Morning
Sun rays on my face
and the morning light fills me
Feeling warm with love
Night
Starshine and moonshine
Twinkling bright in the darkness
Sun awaits its turn

I'm a morning person. Every day I wake up at 5:00 a.m. I love the sunrise and sunshine. Yellow is my favorite color. I love things that sparkle, twinkle, and shine. I'm talking about anything that sparkles. I'm a frosted lipstick person. I actually like glitter.

I'm also drawn to light and to people who radiate it. Have you ever known anyone who radiates positive energy or Light? Are there people in your life who bring sunshine into a room with them? People are drawn to them because they feel their warmth. They see the Light in others and in themselves. I like the expression, "The Light in me honors the Light in you." Try substituting the word "love" for "Light." Or God. You might resonate with that more.

Do you notice how light, or lack thereof, affects your mood? How do you feel after two weeks of gray, rainy days? Some people are gray, rainy day people. It's difficult to be around them for long periods of time. They drain us of energy. Conversely, people who bring light to us energize us.

Now, you might be saying to yourself, "You can get too much sunshine." The light in people isn't dangerous, nor is it forceful. People who have that inner Light radiate and draw you to them. Let's call them Light Workers. Or Love Workers.

My family saw me as sunshine and labeled me Mary Sunshine. I was a bubbly, happy baby and young child–until about the age of five when I'd been given some very negative labels. Labels can be either complementary or limiting, and sometimes they can be cruel.

Labels are never a good idea. They don't take into account that we evolve as human beings. Anytime I showed a negative emotion, I would hear, "Where's our Mary Sunshine? We want her to come back." Labeling other people isn't fair to them. Even if it's a positive label. For example, has anyone ever said to you, "You're such a positive person!" I have, and I usually respond, "Yes, but only on my good days!"

As I've said before, as children, my siblings and I were not allowed to show negative emotions. If we did, we were told to find a way to snap out of it. Remember "Go to your room and don't come out until you have a smile on your face."

In retrospect, I'm certain that I had clinical depression by the time I was 13. I resented the times that they summoned Mary Sunshine to appear when all I wanted to do was cry. As years passed, Mary Sunshine was no longer always shining. I became moody and withdrawn from my family. I immersed myself in school and my social life in which I didn't feel as depressed. I was able to talk with a couple of very close friends about my family and how unhappy I was. They didn't fully believe me. My parents were considered wonderful people in the eyes of our community and church. They appeared to be perfect parents because they were raising such great kids!

For many years, I buried these emotions, and as a result, food became my escape. My salve. My comfort. It wasn't until many years later that I learned how to deal with my negative emotions, especially anger. Thank goodness for therapy and a loving husband. I learned that there was Light in the midst of darkness–that night was as beautiful as day, but in a different way. I loved looking at the stars at night and saw them as tiny Lights against a black velvet sky. And then there's the silver of the moon–an ever-changing Light in itself.

When I was in my late forties, I began to do corporate presentations on professional image and nonverbal communication. I was often asked to speak to professional organizations as well, especially on business dress, using a great slide presentation. I also led workshops on how to use nonverbal communications to be more effective in negotiating.

At the same time, I was adding color analysis to help women know which makeup and clothing would look best on them. I was once asked to color analyze a horse! This was a show horse and the owner wanted to be sure that the blanket and the outfit that the rider wore were the best colors for the horse! Just in case you're curious, the horse was a "winter"!

I also had a great tool to help women know how to dress for their body type and personality: the Personal Image Profile. All these tools were products by a company by the name of BeautiControl. I hated that name. It was a real 1980s and 1990s thing. Image was very important to me, and it still is in some arenas. It's becoming less important to me, as I age. It was a really strong script from my mother!

Over the years, my presentations became more humorous, and I was told by many people how funny I was. A couple of people even said I was a humorist. I had to look that up in the dictionary.

hu ·mor ·ist
/ˈ(h)yo͞omərəst/
noun—

1. a humorous writer, performer, or artist.
2. "the world's best humorists and cartoonists"

Well, I decided that's what I was–a humorist. Think Dave Barry, Erma Bombeck, Mark Twain. Then I fine-tuned my self-description to be an inspirational humorist, because I always interspersed heartfelt stories in my presentations. I had a persona in mind: a crazy, silly version of myself who had very few filters. She could say outrageous things that were funny, but sometimes borderline inappropriate. It was okay because it wasn't really me!

I brainstormed names for her and thought about Mary Sunshine. It didn't sound right, nor did it fit who I was anymore. I'd grown up. I thought about the song *Good Morning Starshine* from the musical, *Hair*. OMG, that's it! Mary Starshine was the integrated, crazy, inappropriate side of me, and that became my outrageous persona who would wear a crazy hat!

I love the idea of Light in the midst of darkness. Stars in the midst of night. Starshine–a balance of my childhood joy and my adult ability to shine in the midst of darkness, metaphorically, my darkness being my depression and finding my way out into the Light…AND the Light within.

By the mid-nineties, I was invited to speak at more state and national association workshops and eventually gave keynote addresses at national events–for $2,000 a pop. I was a member of the prestigious National Speakers Association, where my favorites were Liz Curtis Higgs and Jeannie Robertson. Loretta LaRoche also makes me laugh! Check them out on YouTube. I didn't copy them, but I learned how to craft my own style from watching their skills in crafting their own. My reviews were glowing. I thought that I was in my element. I sure as hell was having loads of fun!

The following is one of my signature pieces. That means I'm known for it being original with me. And memorable. Here's how it works. I have seven sealed envelopes with these answers inside. I ask for a volunteer to reveal the answer when I say "open the envelope." I say something like, "What do you think is the number seven reason that folks can't, or don't want to, or refuse to lighten up? Let's give Carol a drum roll as she opens the envelope!" Each answer is always a fun surprise. There is lots of fun banter in between. And I always have a silly comment or story following each one of these answers. We build up to the number one reason and I don a crab hat and put on a crabby face. They love it!

Mary Starshine's Top 7 Reasons Why Folks Can't Lighten Up

7. They think laughing is morally wrong.

6. If they laugh they might have a heart attack.

5. They lose control when they laugh. Perfect people don't lose control.

4. They would be embarrassed if their teeth fall out when they laugh.

3. They take themselves too seriously. They think laughing is a waste of time.

2. If they laugh too hard, they might pee their pants.

1. They have to give up being crabby.

I needed to work with speakers' bureaus because I really didn't have enough speaking engagements beyond the referrals and repeats I got. I simply wasn't making enough money to consider it a living. Bill was supporting this dream of mine while he was doing software consulting, bless his heart. In order to work with speakers' bureaus, I needed a promo DVD (video at the time), and it was going to cost me about $7,000 to produce a good one. At the same time, the national associations were dwindling in membership, and many of them just shut down. Also, they were drawing from within their own organizations for their keynote speakers.

My presentations were dwindling in numbers as well. I was unable to save the $7,000 for the DVD, and Bill had finished the Y2K influx of work, and we had no health insurance or adequate income, SOOOOOOO, Mary Starshine took a hiatus and went into the closet. I went to work full time in the community life (think activities) department of a lovely continuous care retirement community, Kirkland Village, in the Lehigh Valley. I eventually became director of community life for the independent living and personal care residents.

Oh, how I loved that job. I adored the residents. I resonated with them and their families. I sometimes sat with them at their end-of-life time. It was an honor and privilege to be in their presence. During my nine years at Kirkland Village, I realized that my passion was working with elders. I came face to face with their mortality—and my own. My own parents had died in 2000 and 2002, and I treasured the time I spent with both of them during those last couple of years. I also came face to face with my own mortality when my doctor told me I had only 15 years left to live when I was only 55 years old. And, then again with the risks from my brain surgery.

When I retired from Kirkland Village in 2012, Mary Starshine came out of the closet. I joined a wonderful networking group called Networking From the Heart, organized by Gail Hoover, a dynamo woman. What made the group unique was that they did business with integrity, honesty and love. We modeled after Gail, who did everything from her heart, including her real estate business and the Gail Hoover Foundation-https://www.gailhooverfoundation.org. She helped Bill and me sell two houses—at the asking price!

Mary Starshine got some great speaking gigs out of that networking experience, and my name started to get out locally. Keep in mind, however, that the $2,000 keynotes were over. I found myself speaking mostly to small retiree church groups, mother/daughter banquets, and retirement communities, who had smaller budgets!

I found the need for another type of program, and I got creative. I call it Rising Stars: Live Talk Show Series. Imagine being in the audience of a live talk show, being able to ask questions of people who are rising stars: celebrities, community leaders, heroes, and legends! Mary Starshine does not appear at these. Mary Lilley-Thompson does, as the talk show host.

I also became a laughter leader! People laugh when I say that, but I take laughing very seriously. Here is a list of benefits that laughter provides.

The Eight Physiological Aspects of Laughter

When you laugh, and perhaps even when you smile, your brain chemistry changes and orchestrates the way virtually every system of the body is affected in a healthy way.

1. You get a cardiovascular workout. Your heart rate and blood pressure increase at first, just like when you're exercising. Then they drop to normal levels for as long as 45 minutes after the laughter.

2. A recent theory of how blood temperature is affected by facial expression may well account for laughter's euphoria effect.

3. Muscular tension is incompatible with hearty laughter, so you get muscular relaxation.

4. You get a respiratory workout. During hearty laughter, the diaphragm convulses, and you take in more oxygen.

5. Your thymus gland appears to be stimulated, which means your immune system is more active.

6. Laughter can improve sleep.

7. Laughter can improve digestion.

8. Laughter can improve healing.

Did you know that:

Babies are born knowing how to laugh.

Happy babies are healthier babies.

Happy people are healthier people.

When author, political journalist, editor-in-chief of Saturday Review, Norman Cousins, was diagnosed with cancer, and in severe pain he discovered that 10 minutes of laughter gave him two hours of pain-free sleep.

Research supports the notion that the word laughter is a metaphor for all of the pleasant emotions.

Here's something sad: Children laugh about 400 times a day. That's not the sad part. Adults laugh only about eight times a day. That's the very sad part. You can change that. Laugh for no reason. I highly recommend Dr. Madan Kataria's book, *Laugh for No Reason*. He started laughter clubs in Mubai, India, and they have spread all over the world. Also, go to YouTube and search for "laughter yoga."

At this time in my life, Mary Starshine was riding the wave of doing presentations again, leaving trails of Light. Then, something changed.

12

A TRANSFORMATION ON PURPOSE

During November and December 2019, I had two horrible bouts of bronchitis. I had a raging cough that lasted eight weeks. As a result, I damaged a vocal chord. I also developed phlegm in my throat which created the need to clear it every few seconds! It affected my speech. I had trouble talking to the point that I was unable to do presentations.

My best-in-the-Lehigh-Valley ear, nose, and throat doctor, Aaron Jaworek, MD, who was also a specialist in vocal work, told me that he thought it would heal, but it might take a full year. And, of course, that was the first year of the Covid-19 pandemic. I was still clearing my throat every few seconds. We're still not sure of the cause of that. But, my vocal chord didn't heal, and I never got my voice back—not for doing presentations, not for singing. Rough water.

I mourned the loss of my voice, but more importantly, I mourned the loss of Mary Starshine's presentations. And I grieved the loss of Mary Starshine the most. She was the part of me that was the playful child, the crazy, silly, fun persona who could make people laugh and feel good about themselves. I missed her. Rough water.

By March 2021, with the combination of the loss of my professional speaking and singing voice and Covid, I'd fallen into depression. I felt I had no purpose in life. No goals. No dreams. Nothing to look forward to. I had to cancel two much anticipated trips that year. I was sitting in my recliner playing solitaire on my phone for hours–a sure sign of depression for me. I went back into therapy.

One of my best friends, and my "adopted" daughter, Elizabeth Oleksa, is a certified master life coach, and I decided I needed one. I made that decision on purpose. My purpose was to dramatically change my life. I needed to tackle this head on. I yearned to have my life be different, but had no idea how to go about making that happen. Depression does that. It immobilizes us. We barely get through our activities of daily life, like getting dressed. Forget about the house being clean.

Have you ever had a coach of any kind? I never really had. My parents really hadn't been coaches in their parenting process. Being told I had to have good grades was not my idea of coaching. I had no idea that my experience with Elizabeth would transform me as a person. She is young enough to be my daughter, and I had some initial doubts about her being able to relate to my particular circumstance because of our age difference. Well, forget that! Elizabeth was the perfect coach for me. She gave me the ideal combination of positive encouragement and gentle prodding to push forward through the work we had to do. We had a lot of work to do. And we worked really hard. On purpose.

I dedicated my heart, head, and soul to taking advantage of everything Elizabeth offered me in her coaching. I started a bit slowly, with simply doing ta-dah lists every day. These are to-do lists, but you say ta-dah when you check something off your list!

As a result, I became more engaged in life, sometimes writing simple tasks like organizing one shelf in my pantry. Elizabeth gave me a lot of writing exercises, which helped me delve into who I had been, who I was, who I wanted to be, and what I wanted to do. Then came time to write down my dreams, hopes, and plans. This was difficult at first. It was so new to me, but all the work Elizabeth and I did up to this point helped me process this exercise.

Before I share my dreams with you, I want to let you know about Mary Starshine. I discovered that Mary Starshine didn't die. She was hanging out in the closet. I could open the door anytime and be playful. I didn't have to be on a stage to do that. I could leave trails of Light whenever I felt like it. Mary Starshine was a part of me. Always. She's the part of me that feels and emanates Light. By nature, it's what I bring into a room, according to people who know me. I don't work at it. It just is.

Some of this has to do with my feeling Light, goodness, and warmth in my solar plexus. It's very physical for me to feel that. And when I want to draw upon the best of me, I go to that feeling in my solar plexus. Isn't it ironic that solar is an adjective for the sun? We each have this ability. Some people might have to take small steps to feel the Light.

I hold people in the Light. It's part of the Quaker faith to say that instead of praying for them. I've always found that holding someone in the Light was easier to visualize. Some people might be comfortable in thinking of the Light as God or their higher power. Whatever puts you in touch with something greater than yourself, go with that.

So, with the Light within and Mary Starshine a part of me, too, I was ready to look my dreams directly in the eye. On purpose.

I wanted to work with people, especially golden agers. I needed it to be something meaningful–not a job.

Working as a hospice volunteer seemed like the perfect fit for me. I started with Lehigh Valley Hospice in August 2021, and by January 2022, an end-of-life doula course was offered to both the volunteers and staff. I decided to sign up for that training. And now I am certified as an end-of-life doula by Lehigh Valley Hospice!

An end-of-life doula is a trained person who provides non-medical support and comfort to the dying person and their family, which may include education and guidance as well as emotional, spiritual, or practical care.

I recently had a delightful experience with a patient. I came into his room and asked if I could get anything for him: fresh ice water, coffee, a soda.

"How about some wine—a Cabernet in particular?" he asked and then followed this up with, "But I know they don't allow that here (an inpatient hospice unit)!"

"Well, let's just see about that," I said.

I learned from the nurse in charge that a doctor could write an order for wine for that patient, and his family could bring it in for them. When the patient heard this news, he smiled a huge smile and thanked me.

"It's what we do," I said.

If you know nothing about hospice, know this, you can drink some wine if it makes you happy! It's what being an end-of-life doula is all about. Hospice is a great way to see folks who are terminally ill through the end of their lives. I love this meaningful purpose in my life.

The loss of my voice was a bit more difficult to deal with. I got to thinking about my life and how important my voice had been, professionally speaking and also in singing. I was a voice major at Duquesne University and taught elementary music, which meant I sang every day. And loved it. I sang in the Pittsburgh Oratorio Society back in the 1960s and in church choirs for years. I loved that, too.

But there was also the metaphorical voice that expressed my feelings, opinions, thoughts, wisdom, wit, and stories. My voice was my gift, my talent, my words. My presentations were my way of sharing my gifts and words.

Then it hit me. Enter a second dream: I'd write a book! A memoir. I would use the *written* word as my voice.

You are holding in your hands the result of that dream. Writing a book was a dream of mine about 40 years ago, and I shelved that idea then because I didn't think I had what it takes to write one. The next step was to write a plan for this dream to come true. I'm so grateful to Elizabeth

Oleksa for having this vision for me and coaching me in such a loving way. She is a miracle worker as a coach. It took me some time to actually believe I could do it, but here it is. Dreams can come true.

I encourage you to grab one of your dreams and kick ass to make it come true! On purpose.

13

LEAVING TRAILS OF LIGHT

I love the gospel song, *This Little Light of Mine*. And would we put it under a bushel? No! Would we blow it out? No! These words speak to me. I'm hoping they will also speak to you.

At this point in my life, I have the comfort and confidence of knowing I can leave trails of Light whenever I want to. So, what does it mean to leave a trail of Light? It means that the Light we have inside of us radiates to benefit either a person or place. Just by being kind and thoughtful, we're leaving trails of Light.

Were you ever a Girl Scout? Scouts learn that we need to leave a place or person better than how we found them. Here's an example of how you can easily leave a trail of Light for a person: You're at the grocery store checkout. Always call the associate by their name. Be sure to thank them for their hard work, because it IS hard to stand on your feet all day! Say goodbye using their name. Tell them to take care. You've just left a trail of Light.

It's so darn easy to do. We leave trails of Light so others might feel better. What are some other ways that we can leave trails of Light and make things (people) better than before?

Sometimes we leave trails of Light so others might see their way. Think of a lighthouse with a beacon of light flashing so that ships can navigate without crashing into the rocky shoreline. Here's an example: a friend calls you needing some advice about her alcoholic husband. Your advice to her could be that you steer her to an Al-Anon meeting and give her a contact phone number. That's being a beacon of Light for your friend. Can you think of other ways to be a beacon of light so others might see their way? Warning: Being a beacon of Light is not a way to fix people. It's a way to steer them, to guide them, to coach them. To love them.

I like to call people who leave trails of Light "Light Workers." These are people who radiate Light on purpose–to make the world a better place. If this all feels new to you, just remember the Random Acts of Kindness from the 1970s, or was it the 1980s? Here is a list of several of those types of acts of kindness, which are all beautiful ways to leave trails of Light.

1. Write a positive email.
2. Bike to work.
3. Bake something for your neighbor.
4. Write a positive online review.
5. Donate used books to your library or community center.
6. Hold a door open.
7. Organize a cleanup event.

8. Get a reusable water bottle.
9. Send a care package.
10. Smile more.
11. Call a friend you haven't talked with in a long time.
12. Shovel someone else's sidewalk or parking space.
13. Send an "I'm thinking of you" card.
14. Help someone load their groceries into their car.
15. Offer to do your adult child's laundry.
16. Hold someone in the Light who needs extra care and loving.
17. Hold someone who is different from you in the Light.
18. Take a class in overcoming racial discrimination.
19. Buy lemonade from a child's lemonade stand.
20. Tip generously when warranted.
21. Write your significant other a love note.
22. Give extra hugs to your children.
23. Leave a bag of groceries on someone's porch. Ring the bell and run.
24. Give a shoulder massage to someone you love.
25. Call a friend or family member to tell them you love them.
26. Plant a tree.
27. Donate food to a food bank.
28. Use LED light bulbs.
29. Weed your garden.
30. Give a grocery gift card to a family in need.
31. Smile at everyone you pass in the store or on the street.

NOW IT'S YOUR TURN. WRITE DOWN SOME OF YOUR OWN ideas. Maybe even think about doing one of these a day for the next 31 days! These things have a ripple effect on others, your neighborhood, community, country, and world. Leaving trails of Light could become a world-wide movement! It starts with you and me.

Do you sometimes feel that your "shine" is too bright? Do you think you put people off by shining your Light? Never put it under a bushel! There's a difference between being an out-of-control pollyanna who glares with Light. That puts people off. Think of *radiating* Light rather than *glaring* Light. Or think of *being* the Light. Get it? If it helps to think of God within you, think that. If you can visualize a radiant Light within you, then think that. Whatever is in you that radiates is your best self. My best self honors the best self in you. My heart honors the heart in you. The Light in me honors the Light in you.

My last dream is for you to pass this book on to a friend or family member. One of the best ways to Leave a Trail of Light is to pass it on! Or buy a bunch of books and give them as gifts! Mary Starshine shouted that from the closet!

Holding you in the Light.

RESOURCES

Authors and Speakers

- Mary Lilley-Thompson: www.marystarshine.us
- Starshine Lights The Way – Facebook group page: www.facebook.com/groups/835974173465073
- Mary Starshine, Humorist, author – Facebook page: www.facebook.com/gomarystarshine
- The Self Discovery Advisor – Elizabeth Oleksa, BA, Master Life Coach, poet: www.theselfdiscoveryadvisor.com
- Bright Communications – Jennifer Bright, founding CEO, publisher, editor: www.brightcommunications.net
- Kristin Pedemonti – Storyteller, author, coach, Narrative Therapist: www.steeryourstory.com
- Anne Lamott - Author, inspiration: www.annelamott.com

- Loretta LaRoche – humorist, author, stress expert: www.lorettalaroche.com
- Liz Curtis Higgs – Encourager, Christian humor, author, inspiration: www.lizcurtishiggs.com

Services

- Specialty Moves by Design - Jill Kearney, full service home transitions, Lehigh Valley: www.specialtymovesbydesign.com
- Penny Rhodes – Home Funeral Guide: www.naturalundertaking.org

Other

- Ehlers Danlos Syndrome: www.mayoclinic.org/diseases-conditions/ehlers-danlos-syndrome
- Toxic Positivity: Kendra Cherry: https://www.verywellmind.com/what-is-toxic-positivity-5093958
- The Gail Hoover Foundation: https://www.gailhooverfoundation.org
- Kirkland Village, Continuous Care Retirement Community: www.presbyterianseniorcare.org/Kirkland-Village
- Virginia Ellen, pottery and jewelry: https://artistsatheart.com

ACKNOWLEDGMENTS

A special thanks to my family for being so supportive of my writing this book. They each helped with giving creative critique. Brother Bill, thanks for being the family calendar!

A very special thanks to my husband, Bill, who always believes in me and supports me. Thanks for your editing help! And thanks to Jessica for the honest input to her chapter.

Thanks to Elizabeth Oleksa, certified master life coach, who miraculously helped me transform my life. If it weren't for her, this book would still be a vague dream.

I would like to acknowledge all my Starshiner friends on Facebook, who bring Light and laughter to an ever-growing circle of friends on our Starshine Lights the Way group page. https://www.facebook.-com/groups/835974173465073 Thank you!

Finally, a special thanks to Jennifer Bright, founding CEO of Bright Communications, my editor, book mentor, book doula, hand-holder, and new friend. Without you, the publishing of this book would never have happened so fast! You are a miracle worker.

ABOUT THE AUTHOR

Mary Lilley-Thompson, an inspirational humorist, a laughter leader, author, and human being, is a graduate of Duquesne University, in Pittsburgh, Pennsylvania, with a bachelor of science degree in Music Education, voice major, piano minor. She worked for Westinghouse Electric Corporation, a Fortune 100 company, in a high-powered male-dominated career, which culminated in her becoming an executive with WESCO, Westinghouse Electric Supply company.

A nationally known professional speaker, Mary has more than 25 years experience and was noted as one of the "The Hottest Rising Speakers" in *Adult Ed Today* Magazine.

Mary's careers range from teaching rhythm and movement at the Western Pennsylvania School for the Deaf, and swimming to the physically challenged, at Camp Lend-A-Hand, an Easter Seal Camp, to being the director of community life at a continuous care retirement community, Kirkland Village, in Bethlehem, Pennsylvania. Mary taught music in the Penn Hills school district in Pittsburgh, Pennsylvania, along with teaching more than 45 private piano and voice students. She sang with the Pittsburgh Oratorio Society and created and directed the Beacon Choir of the Unitarian Universalist Church of the Lehigh Valley for a number of years. Mary is a volunteer end-of-life doula for Lehigh Valley Hospice.

Mary has a daughter, two stepsons, five grandchildren, and two great granddaughters. She is retired and lives in the Lehigh Valley, Pennsylvania, with her husband, Bill, and her cat, Meercat.

CPSIA information can be obtained
at www.ICGtesting.com
Printed in the USA
BVHW050305070522
636176BV00006B/18